Minding the Good Ground

Minding the Good Ground
A Theology for Church Renewal

JASON E. VICKERS

BAYLOR UNIVERSITY PRESS

Cover Design by Cynthia Dunne, Blue Farm Graphics
Cover Image © iStockphoto.com / Iain Sarjeant

Library of Congress Cataloging-in-Publication Data

Vickers, Jason E.
Minding the good ground : a theology for church renewal / Jason E. Vickers.
153 p. cm.
Includes bibliographical references (p. 129) and index.
ISBN 978-1-60258-360-3 (pbk. : alk. paper)
1. Church renewal. I. Title.
BV600.3.V53 2011
262.001›7--dc22
2011004657

Printed in the United States of America on acid-free paper with a minimum of 30% pcw recycled content.

For McKenna

Table of Contents

Behold, there went out a sower to sow: And it came to pass, as he sowed, some fell by the way side, and the birds of the air came and devoured it up. And some fell on stony ground, where it had not much earth; and immediately it sprang up, because it had no depth of earth: But when the sun was up, it was scorched; and because it had no root, it withered away. And some fell among thorns, the thorns grew up, and choked it, and it yielded no fruit. And other fell on good ground, did yield fruit that sprang up and increased; and brought forth, some thirty, and some sixty, some a hundred. He said unto them, He that has ears to hear, let him hear.

Mark 4:3-9, KJV

Acknowledgments

It is with deep gratitude that I acknowledge all those who have inspired and supported this volume from its initial conception through publication. The strengths of the volume are theirs; the weaknesses are mine.

First, I am grateful to the faculty, staff, and students of United Theological Seminary, Dayton, Ohio. Among my administrative and faculty colleagues at United, I especially want to thank Wendy Edwards for her leadership in the formation and development of our church renewal program. I also want to thank all the students who have helped to refine my thinking about renewal in the Foundations for Church Renewal course these past four years. Without my colleagues and students at United, I would not have conceived of, much less written, a book on church renewal.

Second, I would like to thank Billy Abraham, Doug Koskela, Dave Watson, and Andy Wood for their timely feedback on portions of the manuscript. I also want to thank my research assistant, Jono Franklin, for his diligent work in tracking down sources, editing the endnotes, and preparing the bibliography and index for this volume.

Third, I am grateful to the editorial, production, and marketing teams at Baylor University Press for the considerable time and talents that they have given to this project. I want to say a special thank you to Carey Newman for his editorial feedback and for challenging me to think from a different angle about church renewal. While I grew weary of rewriting entire sections of the manuscript, his relentlessness about conceptual matters helped to make this a substantially better book.

Finally, I cannot sufficiently express my gratitude to my family for their patience and support during the writing of this volume, and for providing me with the best distractions imaginable, including trips to playgrounds, JDs custard stand, and Memaw and Papaw's mountain house, as well as marathon sessions of Super Mario Brothers devoted to that most important of tasks, getting out of Big Bowser's castle alive! And for the biggest distraction of all, McKenna Eve Vickers, who arrived in time to help me get a 4 a.m. start every morning during the early writing phase, well, this one's for you!

Introduction

Nay, I have doubted whether that arch-heretic, Montanus, was
not one of the holiest men in the second century.

—John Wesley

In 1963 E. R. Dodds, an Ulsterman from County Down, poet and personal friend of T. S. Eliot, and the Regius Professor of Greek at Oxford, gave a brilliant series of lectures at Queen's University Belfast in Ireland. In his lectures, Dodds described the world of early Christianity as "an age of anxiety."[1] Dodds' brilliance, however, lay not in discerning that the early centuries of Christian history were marked by anxiety, but in his attention to the effects of that anxiety on the religious experiences of pagans and Christians alike. Thus he depicted an age brimming with visions and dreams, as well as with asceticism and possession. In other words, the age of anxiety was also an age of *prophecy*.

But there was another side to Dodds' account of early Christian history. If the age of anxiety gave rise to prophets and prophecy, then it also helped to create a drive for orthodoxy and order. "At the beginning of the period," said Dodds, "neither pagan nor Christian thought formed a closed or unified system." Indeed, Christians "were split

1

into many warring sects, which had little or nothing in common save the name of Christian." There was "as yet no authoritative Christian creed nor any fixed canon of Christian scripture."² Beginning in the third century, however, Christians became increasingly determined to mark off orthodoxy from heresy and to establish rules for ordering both their worship and their lives. Thus the age of anxiety was also an age of *structure*.

What was most compelling about Dodds' account of early Christianity was the subtle way in which he kept the prophetic and the priestly structure in constant tension with one another. For example, Dodds told his audience of a second-century prophetess known by Tertullian to converse "with angels and sometimes even with the Lord," and of children known by Cyprian to have "visions and auditions sent by the Holy Spirit, not only in sleep but in waking states of *ekstasis*." But he also reminded them that the Holy Spirit whispered to Ignatius, "Do nothing without the Bishop."³

In the tension between prophets and those who represented structure in the early church, the representatives of structure eventually won out. Thus when Montanus, a Christian prophet who claimed that God was speaking through him, scolded the bishops for their moral and spiritual laxity, the bishops promptly excommunicated him and exorcised evil spirits from his followers. And it was in vain that Tertullian protested that the church was not "a collection of Bishops" and that Irenaeus pled "against the expulsion of prophecy."

Dodds' concluding reflections on the Montanist controversy were both insightful and illuminating:

> From the point of view of the hierarchy the Third Person of the Trinity had outlived his primitive function. He was too deeply entrenched in the New Testament to be demoted, but he ceased in practice to play any audible part in the counsels of the Church. The old tradition of the inspired *prophetes* who spoke what came to him was replaced by the more convenient idea of a continuous divine guidance which was granted, without their noticing it, to the principle Church dignitaries. Prophecy went underground, to reappear in the chiliastic manias of the later Middle Ages and in many subsequent evangelical movements.⁴

As Dodds intimated, though the representatives of structure won out in the Montanist controversy and in early Christianity in general, the victory did not lead to a permanent ban on prophecy in the church. On the contrary, prophecy has reemerged time and again throughout Christian history.[5] What is most interesting, if not altogether surprising, is that the reemergence of prophecy, whether in the form of visions and dreams, contemplation and asceticism, or something else altogether, has usually occurred during subsequent ages of anxiety. Also not surprising is the fact that, in seemingly every age of anxiety, a reemergence of the concern for maintaining structure and order (also in various forms) has accompanied the reemergence of prophecy.[6] For example, we can readily see this in the poverty movement associated with St. Francis of Assisi in the late twelfth and early thirteenth centuries, in the Protestant Reformation in the sixteenth century, and in the Methodist and evangelical revivals in the eighteenth century.[7] In each of these cases, we can discern a palpable tension between the prophetic on the one hand, and a growing concern for structure and order on the other.[8]

The primary *presupposition* of this book is that the Western church is presently immersed in yet another age of anxiety.[9] Like previous ages of anxiety, the present age is characterized by pessimism and despair over the current state of the church and by uncertainty and fear about the church's future. As we will see in a moment, dire predictions abound.

However, our current situation is also like previous ages of anxiety in that it is teeming with prophetic figures who are promoting visions and dreams for the church and who are often critical of the church's leadership. Not surprisingly, these prophetic figures, like their predecessors in ages past, frequently find themselves the target of criticism by "Church dignitaries." In other words, we are once again experiencing the tension between the prophetic and the priestly, or between prophecy and structure.

The primary *problem* that this book seeks to address is one that arises anytime the church experiences a tension between prophecy and structure, namely, how to discern the person and work of the Holy Spirit in the life of the church. As it turns out, this problem is two-sided. On the one side, there is a problem of discernment with respect to prophecy. Not everyone who claims to have a vision from

God is a prophet. Like ancient Israel before it, the church has known its fair share of false prophets. At the same time, we would be wise to follow Irenaeus' advice not to ban prophecy altogether simply because we have seen a false prophet or two. After all, the church celebrates prophetic figures from across the generations whose lives and ministries it deems in retrospect to have been divinely inspired. In an age in which visions and dreams abound, we clearly need help discerning true manifestations of the Spirit in the form of prophecy.

On the other side, there is a problem of discernment with regard to the church's structures. During times of extreme pessimism, uncertainty and fear, many people are tempted (partly by the influence and charisma of prophets) to set Spirit and structure wholly against one another. Yet it is far from clear that the Spirit is opposed to structure.[10] On the contrary, we can make a good case that the church's structures are themselves gifts of the Spirit to be received and cherished as means of grace through which we come to know and to love God.[11] To be sure, not everything that passes for structure is a gift for all seasons. Some *charismata* are clearly temporary in that the Spirit appears to have given them for a particular place and time in the life of the church. But other gifts, such as the sacraments, would seem to have a more enduring, even permanent place in the life of the church. In an age in which some are intimating that the Spirit may have withdrawn from certain ecclesial structures, we clearly need to develop an angle of vision from which we can work to identify the presence and work of the Spirit in and through the church's structures.[12]

The primary *purpose* of this book is to provide a theological angle of vision that will help us to navigate better the tension between prophecy and structure in our present age. Amid all the criticism of the church, we need a sober theological vision of the relationship between the Spirit and the church that can help us stave off doubt and despair. Amid all of the prophets promising to lead the Western church out of decay and decline, we need firm theological ground in which to root our thinking and our decision-making. In other words, our task is to provide a theological vision to aid the work of renewal that is already well underway.

Before we begin constructing this vision, we need to do three more things by way of introduction. First, we need to provide justification or grounds for the presupposition that we are living in an age of anxiety. Second, we need to provide an overview of the astonishing number of prophetic figures and movements that have emerged in the Western church in and around the turn of the third millennium. By extension, we need briefly to identify some of the tensions that have arisen between these figures and movements on the one hand and the representatives of church structure on the other. Third, we need to say a word about the author's ecclesial commitments and about the book's intended audience.

The Present Age of Anxiety

Over the relatively short period of fifty years, a series of events has catapulted the Western church from the confident and at times exuberant optimism of the ecumenical movement in the 1960s to a deep and unsettling anxiety that began in the 1980s and that continues to the present day. Clergy, theologians, and other church leaders are clearly troubled about the current state and future of the church. I have personally encountered this anxiety at clergy conferences, at professional theological societies, in seminary classrooms, at a host of clergy and lay leadership gatherings, and at the faith and order commission of the National Council of the Churches of Christ in the USA (NCC). To be sure, we often hear upbeat keynote messages at these events, but the overall mood is anything but positive.

A quick survey of recent theological literature on the church confirms the diagnosis that we are living in an age of anxiety. For example, one prominent theologian recently declared that we are living in the ruins of the church.[13] Another has announced the end of the church.[14] And yet another has suggested that we are already living in a new dark age.[15]

The mood does not change when we turn from professional theologians' assessments of the current state and future of the church to the assessments of pastors and other Christian leaders. On the contrary, dire predictions abound. For example, in the mid-90s, Mike Regele, a prominent church consultant, forecasted the death of the church, predicting that, within twenty-five years, numerous congregations and even entire denominations would disappear.[16] More recently, Julia Duin, a Christian journalist and assistant national editor for *The*

Washington Times, sounded the alarm that a growing number of evangelicals, most notably women and singles, are "quitting church."[17] On the other side of the gender divide, David Murrow, a Christian television producer, recently declared that American men "hate going to church."[18] More broadly, Brian McClaren, a leading evangelical pastor and popular renewal advocate, has claimed that the church has lost its way.[19]

If theologians, pastors, and other Christian leaders are anxious about the current state and future of the church, then they are not without good reasons. In fact, we can readily identify no fewer than eight developments that are fueling their anxiety. In the interest of being realistic about our situation, we should take a moment to identify these developments.

(1) Over the last fifty years, we have witnessed a steep decline in worship attendance and church membership in the West. Report after report has shown that local congregations and entire denominations in North America and western Europe are now in a statistical tailspin. Studies have shown that, in addition to declining worship attendance and church membership, financial giving is down and the morale of the saints is at an all-time low.[20] And while we may be accustomed to associating decline with so-called "mainline" denominations, i.e., the United Methodist, Presbyterian (USA), Episcopal, and Lutheran churches, we should not think that decline is somehow confined to these churches. Recently, a leading sociologist of religion well-known for his work on Pentecostalism observed that factors historically connected with the decline of mainline Protestantism in the mid- to late twentieth century are beginning to show up within Pentecostalism in the postmodern West.[21]

At the local level, the problem of numeric decline is especially troubling. Faithful members of local churches, many of whom are now aging, are heartbroken over the lack of young families in worship on Sunday morning. I have personally talked with many of them.[22] They are genuinely perplexed by what has happened to the churches that they know and love. They yearn for the days when the church nursery was bustling with activity. They mourn an unspeakable loss.

Suffice it to say, the decline in worship attendance and church membership is easily the number one development behind the current anxiety about the Western church. For many, the next seven developments are contributing to the numeric decline. They are also contributing to our anxiety.

(2) Over the last few decades, we have witnessed countless public scandals involving high-profile church leaders. The scandals have ranged from individual improprieties of varying types to deliberate cover-ups of immoral and sinful activities involving officials at the highest levels of church government.[23] From Jimmy Swaggart, Jim Bakker, and Ted Haggard to the growing scandal over pedophile priests in the Roman Catholic Church, public scandals involving church leaders have had an impact on the way that non-Christians view the church. This is especially true for those who are already skeptical about organized religion. In the wake of public scandals, such persons routinely level charges of hypocrisy at the church.[24] They insist that the church is no better than the rest of the world and that the church's ministers are money-grubbing shysters or worse.

(3) Far from realizing the dreams of the ecumenical movement in the 1960s, we have witnessed numerous acrimonious disputes within denominations, some of which have resulted in church splits. For example, beginning in the 1970s and continuing down to the present day, the Southern Baptist Convention has been mired in internal disputes and controversies over the doctrine of inerrancy and church polity issues. These disputes led to the so-called "fundamentalist takeover" of the convention and to the formation of new alliances and quasi-denominations, including the Alliance of Baptists (1987) and the Cooperative Baptist Fellowship (1990).[25]

More recently, disputes over gay marriage and the ordination of non-celibate homosexuals within mainline denominations came to a head when the Episcopal Church elected Gene Robinson, a non-celibate gay priest, to the office of Bishop. In response to Robinson's election, more than six hundred parishes representing approximately 100,000 members left the Episcopal Church to begin a new denomination, the Anglican Church in North America. And while disputes over gay marriage and the ordination of non-celibate homosexuals have not yet led to official splits within other mainline denominations, many church leaders now fear that an obsession with these issues is getting in the way of the work of ministry. Whatever the source of conflict (e.g., homosexuality, inerrancy, or something else altogether), the threat of division in many churches fuels our anxiety regarding the future.

(4) We have wrestled for several decades with the prospects of secularization. We have told ourselves repeatedly that the culture is increasingly secular, that there is a bias against religion in general and against Christianity in particular, and that Christendom is dead.[26] We bemoan the fact that the culture around us is no longer Christian, if it ever was. The result is that we spend enormous amounts of time and energy debating whether the church should enter into a fresh round of attempting to make itself credible to a secular culture (thereby continuing the great modern liberal project associated with Schleiermacher), or whether we should celebrate our status as resident aliens, working to accentuate the differences between Christianity and culture.[27] Regardless of where we go on this front, the sense that the culture is against us contributes to our growing anxiety concerning the current and future state of the church.[28]

(5) We have struggled with the extent to which Western culture now seems to revolve more around entertainment and recreation than religion. On this analysis, the problem is not that people are hardened atheists or secularists.[29] They are simply finding it difficult consistently to make time for the church amidst their other commitments, including watching their favorite television shows, taking their kids to Sunday soccer leagues, attending professional sporting events, going to the movies, and a host of other weekend pleasures.[30] In response, church leaders have had the unenviable task of deciding whether to insist on loyalty to the church over an entire array of entertainment and recreation options or to attempt to entice prospective members to give the church a try by incorporating some of those options into the church's "benefits package" for members. Churches pursuing the latter strategy have done everything from hosting annual Super Bowl parties to starting their own Sunday soccer leagues.[31] Regardless of how we respond, the growing sense that many people view the church as only one of many ways to spend their Sunday mornings is yet another reason that we are anxious about the current and future state of the church.

(6) While we are worrying about secularization and the obsession with entertainment and recreation, we are also increasingly aware of

the influence of other world religions in the West via globalization. We routinely hear that the church is losing "market share" to Islam, Zen Buddhism, and even to new religions. To complicate matters, we know that inclusivism and tolerance are now among the highest values in Western culture. Thus we are ambivalent about attempting to evangelize people who are even marginally affiliated with another religion.[32] Yet we also sense that there is something of a double standard here, insofar as adherents of other religions are not condemned for sharing their faith with Christians. Whatever the cause, our ambivalence about evangelizing non-Christians fuels our anxiety about the future of the church. We know that, in many western European countries, the church that depends on the birth rate of committed Christians is going to be in big trouble in the coming decades.[33]

(7) We are reluctantly beginning to acknowledge that the professionalization of the ministry has both assets *and* liabilities. After more than a century of commitment to higher theological education and to rigorous credentialing processes for clergy, we now see that we may have unwittingly discouraged the laity from active participation in the work of ministry.[34] We are increasingly open to the possibility that Christianity may be more populist than professional.[35] We realize that our preoccupation with the professionalization of the ministry may have had more to do with our desire for intellectual and cultural respectability than with our desire for the things of God.[36] And yet we sense that we are saddled with the structures that we have, including boards of ordained ministry, seminaries, and divinity schools. We are working diligently to reform our ordination processes and our approach to theological education, making both more accessible to a wider range of people.[37] We are also working to rehabilitate lay ministries. Yet, in the midst of it all, we are quietly worrying that these efforts may be too late—that the cultural divide between clergy and laity opened up by the professionalization of the ministry may have done irreparable damage to the church.

(8) Ironically enough, at the same time that the drive to professionalize the ministry was mandating that clergy become highly educated, religious literacy among the general population was plummeting. Studies have shown that, over the last fifty years, fewer and fewer people can name the four Gospels, not to mention the rest of the books of Scripture.[38] And while we have a long way to go toward

understanding the many causes of "religious illiteracy," we sense that we have done a poor job teaching the faith to our children. To be sure, many churches are working to recover the art of catechesis, but we will be playing catch-up for decades to come on this front as well.

We could easily think of more reasons to be anxious about the current state and future of the church in the postmodern West. For example, we might add to the list the transformation of theology from a practical discipline intimately related to the sacramental life of the church to a speculative and scientific discipline struggling to meet the demands of the so-called "hard sciences" in the modern university.[39] However, we have done enough to secure the point that we are living in an age of great anxiety. We must now turn our attention to the prophetic leaders and movements that are heralding new visions and dreams for the church.

Prophetic Leaders and Movements

As noted above, ages of anxiety have, throughout Christian history, yielded an astonishing array of prophetic leaders and movements in the life of the church. Thus we should not be surprised that, amid all of the anxiety and hand-wringing about the current state and future of the church in the postmodern West, a large and growing number of prophetic leaders and movements have appeared on the scene. For example, we now have serious proposals for how to renew the church from Donald McGavran, Pete Wagner, and the church growth movement;[40] Rick Warren and the purpose-driven movement;[41] Darrell Guder, Alan Hirsch, Mike Slaughter, and the missional church movement;[42] Ray Anderson, Tony Jones, Dan Kimball, and the emerging church movement;[43] Shane Claiborne, Jonathan Wilson-Hartgrove, Elaine Heath, and the new monasticism movement;[44] Robert Webber and the ancient-future movement;[45] Neil Cole, Frank Viola, and the organic church movement;[46] Pete Ward and the liquid church movement;[47] Larry Osborne and the sticky church movement;[48] Carol Merritt and the tribal church movement;[49] and Jim Belcher and the deep church movement.[50]

These prophetic leaders and movements have at least four things in common. *First*, they all offer a diagnosis for what is wrong with the church. For example, the church growth, organic church, and tribal church movements tend to criticize the Western church for its failure to present the gospel in ways that are more likely to be recognized, appreciated, and ultimately embraced by a growing secular culture. The missional, the emerging, the new monastic, and the purpose-driven church movements tend to criticize the Western church for its failure consistently to meet the demand of the gospel to care for the orphans and widows of the world. And the ancient-future, emerging, new monastic, and deep church movements frequently criticize the church for leaving behind many of the best insights and practices of the church from across the centuries.

Second, all of the above named prophetic leaders and movements herald dreams and visions for how to fix what is wrong with the church. In every case, the prescription for how to fix the church matches the diagnosis of what is wrong. For example, the church growth, organic church, and tribal church movements all promote ways to reach people "where they are." Similarly, the missional, emerging, new monastic, and purpose-driven movements all urge churches to order their ministries in ways that focus their energies and resources on the most pressing needs of the world. Likewise, the ancient-future, emerging, new monastic, and deep church movements all offer suggestions for recovering what they regard as the best practices and insights from the past.

Third, all of these prophetic leaders and movements transcend denominational boundaries. To be sure, many of these prophetic leaders and movements originate with and often remain associated with local congregations (e.g., Rick Warren and Saddleback Church), but their audience and their influence are rarely, if ever, confined to a particular congregation or even an entire denomination. On the contrary, they host major conferences that are attended by clergy and lay leaders from across a broad spectrum of denominations, and they maintain websites and publish literature that rarely endorse or promote a particular denomination.

Fourth, because these prophetic leaders and movements have such a broad audience, they are not subject to denominational structures or to approval by the relevant "church dignitaries." Though many of the leaders are themselves ordained clergy within particular denominations, their authority is more charismatic than priestly. Consequently, most, if not all, of these prophetic leaders and movements are often the subjects of deep concern on the part of clergy and other church leaders who represent denominational structures. For example, it is not uncommon to hear such persons expressing deep concern over whether a particular prophetic movement coheres well with their theological and liturgical traditions. Moreover, persons who worry about denominational identity are often quick to note that many clergy and churches that have been influenced by these prophetic leaders and movements often deliberately obscure or even leave off their denominational affiliation on church letterhead and worship bulletins. Many are now concerned that local congregations are becoming more missional than Methodist, more purpose-driven than Presbyterian, more emerging than Episcopalian.

For some, what is most troubling is no doubt the degree of influence that these prophetic leaders and movements have in many quarters of the church today. Clergy conferences sponsored by local congregations affiliated with these prophetic movements or featuring one or more of these prophetic leaders have no trouble reaching maximum seating capacity in midsized to large venues.[51] Indeed, these conferences routinely generate more energy and buzz among clergy than either annual denominational clergy gatherings or renewal conferences put on by intradenominational renewal groups.[52]

Beyond worries related to denominational identity and loyalty, vigorous and sometimes heated debate over these prophetic leaders and movements centers on three issues. Most notoriously, there is a vigorous ongoing debate within many local churches and among the clergy of many denominations over what these leaders and movements recommend with respect to worship. Often, this debate is cast in terms of contemporary versus traditional worship, but it is far more complex and controversial than that.[53] For example, when clergy talk about traditional worship, they usually have in mind worship that features hymns sung from hymnbooks with piano and organ accompaniment. When they discuss contemporary worship, they usually mean worship that involves praise choruses and ample use of keyboards, drums, guitars, and other instruments. Yet advocates for the emerging church, the ancient-future church, and the deep church movements often encourage churches to recover things like iconography, Lenten practices, and the regular confession of creeds in worship. For many local congregations, these things are even more controversial than the incorporation of praise choruses, drums, and guitars.

Another area of controversy and debate revolves around what these prophetic leaders and movements have to say about the relationship between the church and the wider culture. On this front, some stress the need for the church to be distinct from the culture, while others urge the church to be more culturally accommodating. Not surprisingly, those prophetic leaders and movements that urge the church to recover ancient liturgical and even ascetical practices often stress the need for the church to remain distinct from the surrounding culture, whereas those that promote more contemporary forms of worship often encourage the church to make ready use of all that the wider culture has to offer.

Finally, we have noted that many of these prophetic leaders and movements are urging the church to be more responsive to the needs of the world, especially to things like hunger and homelessness, HIV/AIDS, and poverty. While few would argue that such work is unimportant, there is much debate about whether or not this vision of the church's mission is too one-sided. Thus some are quick to criticize the missional, purpose-driven, and emerging church movements for their perceived failure to put equal, if not greater, emphasis on things like worship, evangelism, and theological/spiritual formation.

For clergy serving in local congregations, the sheer number of prophetic voices and movements can be overwhelming. Add to this the concern for denominational identity and loyalty, as well as the kind of debates that we have just been outlining, and we can see why many clergy and other church leaders are divided about which, if any, of these prophetic leaders and movements is worth following. Some clergy and local churches resolve the dilemma by aligning themselves almost entirely with one of these prophetic movements. Thus there are local congregations that self-identify as emerging or missional, as deep churches or liquid churches, and so on. Other clergy and local churches refuse to align themselves with any of these prophetic leaders and movements, insisting that they are merely passing fads. Most clergy and congregations, however, fall somewhere in between these two extremes. They are anxious and concerned about their future, and they are aware that the "flagship" congregations of these prophetic movements are thriving in ways that they are not (e.g., financially, in worship attendance, and in service to the community).[54] They know that they must do something if they want to survive for another generation, but they are not sure whom to follow.

My own judgment is that we should celebrate the fact that we are living in an age of so many prophetic leaders and movements. Amid all of our anxiety about the future of the Western church, they are a reason to be hopeful.[55] This is not to say that these movements are beyond criticism. On the contrary, a quick review of prophetic leaders and movements from across church history reveals that almost all of them are intensely, even myopically, focused on a particular area of concern or at best a small nexus of concerns. For example, the poverty movement was intensely focused on caring for the poor, while the Protestant Reformation was intensely focused on recovering the doctrine of justification by faith, a theology of the cross, and the authority of Scripture. In other words, one way to think about prophetic leaders and movements is to see them as the Spirit's means of correction within the life of the church. When the church is neglectful of some aspect of its calling, the Spirit raises up prophetic leaders and movements to call the church to be faithful to that aspect of its calling.[56]

When we think about prophetic leaders and movements as the Spirit's means of correction within the life of the church, two things immediately follow. First, far from dismissing them as mere passing fads, we should work prayerfully to discern what the Spirit may be saying to the churches in and through these leaders and movements. Second, far from looking to these leaders and movements as providing comprehensive visions for the church and for ministry, we need to take a more modest approach, identifying their best insights and then integrating those insights into a more robust theological vision of the church and of ministry.

The chief advantage of this way of thinking about and responding to prophetic leaders and movements is that it allows us to remain genuinely open to the prophetic without being neglectful or even dismissive of time-tested ecclesial structures. On the one hand, this way of thinking requires us to be attentive to the prophetic, working prayerfully to identify the corrective voice of the Spirit in our present age of anxiety. On the other hand, this way of thinking prevents us from mistaking the corrective voice of the Spirit in the form of prophetic leaders and movements for a wholesale condemnation or rejection of the materials, persons, and practices that, over the course of the centuries, have become established and secure in the life of the church.[57] By extension, this way of thinking does not force us to self-identify with one leader or movement. We do not have to abandon our long-standing identities as Methodist, Presbyterian, or Episcopalian to become missional, purpose-driven, or emerging. Rather, we can range far and wide, identifying the best insights and suggestions from among the various prophetic movements now on the horizon and then integrating those insights and suggestions into the wider visions of the church that originate within and reflect the theological traditions to which our local congregations belong.[58]

What is needed, then, is a theological vision of the church *within* which we can begin prayerfully to discern what the Spirit is saying to our churches through the many prophetic leaders and movements surrounding us today, and *into* which we can integrate their best insights and suggestions for how we ought to respond. To provide such a vision is the primary purpose of this book. From time to time, we will have occasion to make observations about some of the renewal movements mentioned above, but our main purpose will be to provide a theological vision of the church that can aid us in the work of assessing the visions and dreams of present and future prophetic leaders and movements and integrating their best insights and suggestions within the ongoing lives of local congregations and even entire denominations.

Now that we have a clear sense of the primary purpose of the chapters up ahead, we need to attend to two more matters by way of introduction. On the one hand, we need to acknowledge the ecclesial location of the author and therefore the argument of this book. On the other hand, we need to say a word about the book's intended audience.

Author and Audience

Works of theological reflection on the church are, with one possible exception, embedded in particular ecclesial communions. Some proposals trade on evangelical Protestant understandings of the church and her ministries, while others reflect Roman Catholic, Eastern Orthodox, Anglican, and Pentecostal understandings.[59] With this in mind, I should say a word about the ecclesial embeddedness of this particular work.

My location in the Wesleyan theological tradition and in a mainline Protestant church has deeply formed the vision of the church in this book. More specifically, the pneumatologically oriented theology of John and Charles Wesley, the pietism and revivalism inextricably woven into the DNA of Methodism, the emphasis on evangelism and conversion that runs through the Methodist tradition, and the concern for personal and social holiness that has characterized all branches of Wesleyanism—all of these things have shaped and guided my thinking about the church.[60] People in other ecclesial settings will no doubt have differing views on some of these matters, but it is my sincere hope that, in the pages that follow, they will find a theological vision of the church that, with appropriate amendments, they can readily deploy in the work of ministry and in the lives of their local congregations.

The one exception to the rule that works on the church are deeply embedded in particular ecclesial traditions may be the recent work on the church undertaken by the World Council of Churches (WCC). By definition, the ecumenical movement is not embedded in one particular denomination or ecclesial tradition. Thus, the work of the World Council of Churches in and around ecclesiology can serve as a check and balance for one's own thinking in this area. Throughout this work, I will therefore show areas of convergence (as well as occasional areas of divergence) between my own views on the church and the views forged through ecumenical dialogue at the level of the WCC. For the latter, I will rely primarily on the work made available in Faith and Order Paper 198, or the document called *The Nature and Mission of the Church: A Stage on the Way to a Common Statement* (hereafter NMC).[61]

Finally, I have written this book as a theological primer for seminary students who are preparing to go into full-time ministry in local congregations. Many seminary students are understandably drawn to prophetic leaders and movements within the contemporary Western church. However, I have found that these movements are often very divisive. Some seminary students are clearly devotees of a particular leader or movement, whereas others are almost entirely dismissive of that same leader or movement. What is missing from the conversation is a theological framework within which to think about these leaders and movements. My main concern, therefore, has been to provide a text that can spur critical and creative thinking about contemporary church renewal movements *from a theological perspective.* It is my sincere hope that persons preparing for ministry (and even persons already well along in their ministerial careers!) will find in the pages that follow a sober way of entering into what is sure to be an ongoing dialogue about the current state and future of the Western church.

Chapter 1

The Nature of the Church

If we are going to develop a theological framework within which we can think about and assess proposals for church renewal, then the most natural place to begin is with the theological discipline known as *ecclesiology*.[1] Having said this, we will not be constructing a full-blown ecclesiology, as such a task would require us to think critically about an entire host of things, including the various offices or orders of ministry and church discipline or canon law.[2] Our goal is more modest. We are setting out to provide a *framework* for thinking about renewal.

By definition, frameworks are not exhaustive or full-blown accounts. They are conceptual schemes or rubrics that can help to guide and to stimulate our thinking about a topic. The construction of a framework therefore typically involves identifying and exploring the concepts or categories in a given area of inquiry that we deem most essential for thinking about more specific matters. Thus, in what follows, we will identify and explore three vital concepts within ecclesiology that are especially crucial for thinking about church renewal, including (1) the nature of the church, (2) the mission of the church, and (3) the sacramental life of the church.

In this chapter, we will be reflecting on the *nature* of the church. We will explore the mission of the church and the sacramental life of the church in the chapters that follow. We will conclude each chapter by showing how and why these concepts are crucial for our thinking about church renewal.

Doing Ecclesiology in an Age of Anxiety

In setting out to think theologically about the church, one of the biggest challenges that we must confront is the fact that we are dealing with a topic about which there is no shortage of assumptions and expectations. People within and outside the church have an endless array of assumptions about what the church is, and an equally endless array of expectations about what the church ought to be doing in the world. For example, when people outside the church accuse the church of hypocrisy, they are giving voice to assumptions and expectations concerning what the church ought to be or not to be and what the church ought to do or not do. Similarly, when local congregations become deeply divided over whether to use their resources to build new schools for children in predominantly Islamic countries or to renovate and expand their own sanctuaries, they are, more often than not, dealing with conflicting assumptions and expectations concerning what the church ought to be and to do in the world.

While the reality of conflicting assumptions and expectations about the church is one that clergy and other church leaders must face in every age, ages of anxiety have a way of exacerbating the situation. When we Christians are deeply worried about the current state and future of the church, we naturally begin thinking and talking about what is wrong with the church and about how to put things right. Unfortunately, our sense of urgency often causes our conversations to become accusatory and inflammatory. Before we know it, we are having bitter disagreements about who is to blame for the decline of the church.

At one level, we can view our disagreements about what is wrong with the church and about how to put things right as a self-critical mechanism within the life of the church that is worthy of celebration. Indeed, a positive way to think about deep disagreements in the church is to see them as an indicator that a significant number of people care enough about the church to argue over what the church should be or what the church should do in the world. In other words, deep disagreements are a better problem to have than apathy or indifference.[3]

At another level, however, the problem with many of our disagreements over what is wrong with the church and over how to put things right is that they often amount to a declaring of our assumptions and expectations about the church in a loud voice. On all sides, there is a regrettable lack of sober theological reflection about the church. We criticize the church and her leaders, we make demands of the church, and in a few cases we even threaten to leave the church. For instance, any pastor who has journeyed with a church through a time of deep disagreement is likely to have experienced people on both sides threatening to leave if x happens or doesn't happen. Similarly, denominations that are deeply divided over an issue routinely have clergy and lay members on both sides threatening to "pull out" if the issue is not resolved in a way that satisfies them.

In an age of anxiety, we need to be particularly wary of doing ecclesiology through a megaphone. It is bad enough that we are deeply worried about the church—that we are afraid for the church's future. When we begin shouting our assumptions and expectations about the church at one another, we only make matters worse.

Amid our growing anxiety about the church, we ought to be doing ecclesiology on our knees.[4] Far from shouting at one another, we need to enter into a round of prayerful reflection on what the church is called by God to be and to do in the world. The proper way to begin this prayerful reflection is not by naming what is wrong with the church or by making a case for how to put things right, and we certainly shouldn't begin by deciding who is to blame. Rather, we should begin by reflecting prayerfully on what sort of community the church is. In other words, the proper place to begin is with *the nature of the church*.

Before we turn our attention to the nature of the church, we should take a moment to justify our claim that this is the proper place to begin our reflections. We can do so by noting two problems that tend to arise when we begin elsewhere, most commonly with the mission of the church. First, while the nature and mission of the church cannot be entirely separated from one another, it is now increasingly common to conflate or confuse the two. Indeed, many churches are so focused on a particular aspect of the church's mission that they rarely take time to think about the sort of community the church is. One of the most prevalent examples of this tendency can be seen in churches that preach and teach that the church is Christ's only hands and feet in the world. Consider the following statement from Mike Slaughter, a leader in the missional church movement and the senior pastor of Ginghamsburg United Methodist Church in Tipp City, Ohio:

> What does it mean to be Christ's body in the world? We as the church are the only hands that Jesus has to rebuild in broken places. Our feet are his only feet to march in the war against poverty and injustice. Our voices are his voice to share the good news of eternal life and offer hope to the hopeless. Our bank accounts are the only fiscal resources he has to carry out the Father's mission.[5]

If this is intended as a statement about the nature of the church, then it is a highly problematic one, tending as it does to blur the line between the church and Jesus Christ or between ecclesiology and Christology. For now, let us give church leaders who make this kind of statement the benefit of the doubt by assuming that they are making a statement about the *mission* of the church. If this is the case, then such a statement will eventually lead to despair and exhaustion if it is not carefully situated against a robust and healthy understanding of the *nature* of the church. Churches will either develop a messiah complex and fall into despair when their best efforts do not solve the world's problems, or staving off despair, they will exhaust themselves financially, spiritually, emotionally, and personally.

The second problem that can arise when we do not begin our reflections with the nature of the church is in the immediate neighborhood. Most proposals for church renewal are really proposals about the mission of the church. When claims about the mission of the church are not carefully rooted in a theological account of the nature of the church, we can quickly forget that the church is not simply a collection of hardworking, self-reliant individuals. We can forget that, while the church is clearly a human institution, it is also divine, which means among other things that her most important resources are the ones that she receives from God. In other words, we can fail to see that our hope ultimately lies not in our own ingenuity and effort but in the presence and power of the Holy Spirit who animates and empowers the church, incorporating her into the Trinitarian life of God.[6]

We could easily identify other problems that can occur when we do not begin with the nature of the church. In lieu of this, we need to begin developing a theological vision of the nature of the church. When we have done so, we will return to the two problems that we have just outlined, indicating how this vision can help to prevent these problems from arising in the first place.

The Marks of the Church

As with any other topic in theology, how we think about the nature of the church will depend on two things. First, it will depend on the kinds of questions we ask at the outset. Second, it will depend on the sources to which we turn in an effort to answer those questions.

With this in mind, one way to begin thinking about the nature of the church is to inquire after its characteristic features or attributes. In other words, we can simply inquire about what the church is like. An analogy will help to show how entirely natural it is to proceed this way. If we want to know about the nature of a particular breed of dog, then we can do worse than to pay attention to what the dog is like by inquiring after its distinguishing features. We will want to know whether the breed is typically energetic or docile, whether it is generally good with children or aggressive and unpredictable, and so on.[7] Suffice it to say, we can take a similar approach when inquiring after the nature of the church. To do so, we need only to acquire a list of the church's distinguishing features.

In order to pursue this strategy, we must decide where we should look to acquire a list of the distinguishing features of the church. Initially, we might wish to proceed empirically, identifying and listing the characteristic features of the particular churches to which each of us belongs. Unfortunately, if we go this way, we will have to build a massive database to store the list of features that each church will generate. Such a list will quickly become unmanageable. We will have so many distinguishing features that it will be virtually impossible to assimilate or coordinate them into a coherent vision of the nature of the church. If we are to make progress on this front, then we are going to need a more manageable source from which to begin our reflections.

Fortunately, we do not have to invent a list of the church's distinguishing features from scratch. On the contrary, we can rely on two sources that reveal to us what our ancestors in the faith identified as the distinguishing features of the church. On the one hand, we can turn to the official dogmatic and doctrinal statements contained in the Nicene Creed and in classical Protestant confessions of faith and/or articles of religion.[8] On the other hand, we can turn to the New Testament.[9] Let us see what these sources have to say about the distinguishing features of the church. Once we have identified the distinguishing features of the church in each of the sources, we will inquire about whether they really capture and convey the true nature of the church.

At first glance, the Nicene Creed appears ready-made for our purposes, containing as it does a short list of notes or marks of the church. According to the Nicene Creed, the church is "one holy catholic and apostolic."[10] When we turn to the classical Protestant confessions of faith and articles of religion, the list is even shorter, consisting of two distinguishing features. According to most Protestant confessions of faith and articles of religion, the church is the place where (1) the pure word of God is preached and (2) the sacraments are duly administered.

When we turn from Protestant confessions of faith and from the Nicene Creed to the New Testament, things immediately get messier. In lieu of tidy lists of distinguishing features, the Scriptures offer a range of vivid images and metaphors for the church.[11] For example, the New Testament depicts the church as the body of Christ, a city on a hill, a light to the world, the branches of the true vine, and the spotless bride of Christ to name just a few. To be sure, these Scriptural images are striking and highly suggestive. For example, they suggest that the church is the sort of community that helps the world to find its way out of darkness, that offers a place of safe haven for weary travelers, and that maintains spiritual and moral purity. At the same time, the New Testament metaphors for the church are not as straightforward as the descriptions of the church in the Nicene Creed or in Protestant confessions of faith and articles of religion. As with all metaphors, there is the problem of interpretive elasticity.[12] We can easily bend these biblical metaphors in any number of directions.[13]

For the time being, let us grant that there is a range of interpretive possibilities for the metaphors in the New Testament and even for the terms used in the Creed and Protestant confessions. Moreover, let us grant that, in what follows, we will be making some assumptions concerning the meaning of the relevant terms and metaphors. We can readily grant these things because what really matters for the sake of the argument is that both our initial and concluding judgments concerning the *adequacy* of these metaphors and terms will hold even if we allow for a range of meanings.[14]

Having identified the lists of distinguishing features of the church in the Nicene Creed and in Protestant confessions of faith, we now need to discern whether these lists adequately or truly describe the church in its many manifestations across space and time. Likewise, we need to ascertain whether the images and metaphors for the church in the New Testament really capture what the church is like throughout the history of the church and in the present day. In other words, we need to know whether the church, then or now, really is one, holy, catholic, and apostolic. Alternatively, we need to know whether the church, then or now, truly is a city on a hill, the branches of the true vine, and the body of Christ. If it turns out that the descriptions of the church in the Creed, in Protestant confessions, and in the New Testament do not match what we actually see and experience of the church throughout space and time, then we will have no choice but to conclude initially that these descriptions do not adequately describe the church's true nature.[15]

Before we evaluate the descriptions of the church in the Nicene Creed, the Protestant confessions, and the New Testament for their adequacy, a brief word of warning is in order. Our initial judgment will strike many readers as unduly negative. Here we can only ask for patience. As we will note in a moment, there are good reasons to acknowledge the church's many failings across the years. More importantly, our *initial* judgment concerning the adequacy of the descriptions will not be our *final* judgment. On the contrary, we will in due course maintain that, when viewed from a particular theological angle of vision, the descriptions are indeed adequate or true. For now, the time has come to offer an initial judgment concerning whether the descriptions appear at first glance adequately or truly to describe the nature of the church across space and time.

Those who love the church deeply will want to insist that, whatever her imperfections, the church really is one, holy, catholic, and apostolic. We will maintain that, whatever her shortcomings might be, the church really is a light to the world, the spotless bride of Christ, and a royal priesthood descended from David. We will insist that someone is always preaching the pure word of God and duly administering the sacraments. After all, we will say, God will not be without a witness in the world.

Even those of us who love the church and who give the whole of our hearts and lives in her service know better. Whatever our ideal and ethereal visions of the church might be, the historical and present realities of the church's life are extremely difficult to ignore. No one knows this better or is pained by it more than those who truly love and faithfully serve the church. For example, concerning present realities in the church, Hughes Oliphant Old laments, "That the church is the bride of Christ, without spot or wrinkle, seems to be a faded vision. The purity of the church is an increasing problem. Many of us find ourselves belonging to churches that countenance practices quite contrary to historic Christian teaching."[16]

Consider the ways in which the church has failed to live up to the marks of the church in the Creed. We know that the church is not truly one.[17] On the contrary, we know only too well that the church has been deeply divided and disunited across space and time. To be sure, some representatives of the Eastern Orthodox and Catholic churches will want to maintain that church unity has persisted across space and time within their respective communions. Yet, for this argument to hold, they will eventually need to deny the legitimacy of other churches. Orthodox Christians will have to deny the legitimacy of Catholic and Protestant churches, and Catholic Christians will have to deny the legitimacy of Orthodox and Protestant churches.[18]

Short of such denials, we simply cannot ignore the disunity that exists among the various churches of the world. For us Protestant types, the problem of disunity is especially bad, as our various communions are notorious for internal division and schism, not to mention for their lack of unity with either Catholic or Orthodox churches. For example, Lutheran, Reformed, Baptist and Methodist communions have fragmented and splintered repeatedly across the years. Indeed, despite the recent ecumenical dialogue between Protestant churches on the one hand and the Catholic and Orthodox churches on the other, Protestant families themselves often remain bitterly divided. Thus we are more likely to witness ecumenical dialogue between the United Methodist Church and the Roman Catholic Church or the Lutheran Church than between the United Methodist Church and the wider Wesleyan and pan-Methodist family of churches of which it is purportedly a part. Blood may be thicker than water, but the division that results from family feuds may be deeper and more difficult to overcome than division between altogether different families.

We also know that the church is not holy. However we finesse the definition of holiness, we cannot ignore the church's failings on this front. If holiness has to do with being set apart, we can readily think of numerous occasions on which the church failed adequately to distinguish itself from the wider culture.[19] Similarly, if holiness has to do with keeping the moral law of God, then we can readily think of occasions when the church (or at least the church's members) has broken God's laws.[20]

We know too that the church is not catholic. Across space and time, the church has on more than one occasion failed to be welcoming and hospitable to all persons. In the worst instances, the church has deliberately excluded persons from her services on the basis of race, ethnicity, social class, and the like.

Finally, with regard to the marks of the church in the Nicene Creed, we know the church is not apostolic. For example, there are at least two major ways to understand the meaning of apostolic. On the one hand, we can think of apostolicity in a literal way, having to do with an unbroken line of bishops and ordination stretching from Peter to the present pope. On the other hand, we can think of apostolicity in terms of continuity of teaching or doctrine, having to do with handing on the teaching of the apostles from generation to generation. Either way, any claim to apostolic succession or continuity across space and time is bound to run into numerous problems. Showing an unbroken line of bishops and ordination is notoriously problematic, and any notion of word-for-word continuity of teaching and doctrine across the centuries is highly presumptive at best.[21]

The problem does not go away when we turn to the description of the church on offer in Protestant confessions of faith and articles of religion. The history of preaching is full of examples of the life-giving power of the word of God. It is also full of manipulation and abuse. Moreover, if we take the classical Protestant confessions in their historical context seriously, then we must recall that, from the perspective of the Reformers, the Reformation was necessary precisely because there was a widespread failure on the part of the late-medieval Catholic Church to preach the pure word of God and to administer the sacraments duly.

The church does not fare better when her life is compared to the metaphors and images of the church in the New Testament. Across space and time, the church's record is checkered at best. As often as not, the church has failed to be light and salt in the world. As often as not, the church has hidden the light of Christ under a bushel rather than holding it high on a hill for all to see. As often as not, the church's branches have withered and died rather than bearing fruit worthy of the true vine.

The list of the church's spiritual and moral failings across the centuries is well-known, and I have deliberately avoided rehearsing it here.[22] My intention is to encourage *realism* about the nature of the church, not skepticism, suspicion, and sarcasm. In the present age, there is more than enough of the latter to go around. If we encourage radical skepticism about the church or embrace a hermeneutics of suspicion that goes all the way down, then we will set the bar too low in our quest for church renewal. We will expect next to nothing from the church, and we will get next to nothing in return. Yet realism is desperately needed in our thinking about the church. Without a healthy dose of realism, we will set the bar too high, developing visions of the church that no congregation can realize.

If the descriptions of the church in the Nicene Creed, the Protestant confessions of faith, and the New Testament are historically problematic, then there is also a significant *practical* problem. Indeed, to claim that the church today is one, holy, catholic, and apostolic or that the church is the spotless bride of Christ is to risk one of two problematic responses. On the one hand, we will embrace the claim and ignore the church's present shortcomings and failings, however grotesque. Such a response entails being willfully dishonest about our life together and refusing to confess our collective sins. Let us call this response *denial*.

On the other hand, we will acknowledge the claim, but we will become cynical and bitter about the church as we actually experience it. The discrepancies between the marks of the church and the reality of the church as we know it will drive us to adopt an unholy trinity of skepticism, suspicion, and sarcasm. Let us call this response *despair*.

It would be a great mistake to think that these are not real problems in the church today. Sadly, many clergy and laity alike readily succumb either to denial or despair. In the worst cases of denial, clergy and laity ignore or even cover up horrific forms of evil in the church, including financial, emotional, and even sexual abuse.[23] In the worst cases of despair, clergy and laity give up on a gospel according to which genuine redemption and change is possible here and now in favor of a gospel of radical pessimism and skepticism about human persons and communities.[24] Thus we either ignore our sins entirely or wallow in them like filthy swine.

Given the historical and practical problems that emerge when we compare the church with the descriptions of the church in the Nicene Creed, the Protestant confessions, and the New Testament, perhaps we should try another approach. After all, the process so far has led us to say more about what the church is *not* than about what the church *is*. If we are to get around this problem, then we are going to have to think about the nature of the church from a different angle, namely, *in light of the church's origins*. Once we consider the nature of the church in light of the church's origins, we will make a case that we can truly ascribe to the churches that we know and love all that is said of the church in the Nicene Creed, in Protestant confessions of faith and articles of religion, and in the New Testament.

The Pentecostal Origins of the Church

The question of the origins of the church is not an uncontested one. Some locate the origins of the church with the first disciples of Jesus or with Jesus himself, taking seriously, if not literally, the notion that the church is the body of Christ. Others push the origins of the church back even further, taking seriously, if not literally, the metaphor of the church as the new Israel. If the church is the new Israel, then in some sense the church must be said to originate with ancient Israel.

Neither of these ways of understanding the origins of the church is without problems. For example, if we draw too intimate a connection between the church and Jesus Christ, then we will constantly run the risk of overlooking the utter uniqueness of the person and work of Jesus. We will be prone to confuse the work of the church with the saving work of Christ, regarding ourselves in a wooden and all too literal way as the hands and feet of Christ. In doing so, we will constantly risk forgetting that it is Christ's body that is broken and Christ's blood that is shed for the salvation of the world. However we may wish to understand the church as the body of Christ, we must be careful not to confuse the church with the body broken once and for all as an atoning sacrifice for the forgiveness of sins. Directly to equate the origins of the church with the coming of Christ or even with the life of Christ is to risk the development of a messiah complex on the part of the church. The church bears witness to and celebrates the coming of the Messiah, but she is not the Messiah.

Similarly, to suggest that the church originates with Israel is to overlook the uniqueness of Israel both historically and presently. How exactly to understand the relationship between the church and ancient Israel is a thorny issue, and we will not be able to resolve it here.[25] Suffice it to say that equating the origins of the church with ancient Israel may very well be unjust both to ancient Israel and to the church. From the standpoint of ancient Israel, such a move is anachronistic at best. From the standpoint of the church, such a move distracts from the unique circumstances in which the church *as such* originated.

In lieu of the foregoing ways of thinking about the origins of the church, I suggest that we take seriously the notion that the church as such began at Pentecost.[26] To that end, what follows is a historical-theological retelling of the pentecostal origins of the church. It is historically oriented insofar as it has to do with the events that took place at a particular date and time and in a particular location, namely, nine in the morning on the day of the Jewish pilgrimage and harvest festival known as *Shavuot* in the city of Jerusalem. It is theologically oriented insofar as it provides a constructive and imaginative understanding of what took place just before, during, and immediately after that day.

The story of Pentecost is a familiar one. For children and adults not baptized in the waters of modern skepticism and doubt, Pentecost readily captures and fires the imagination. Out of nowhere comes a violent rushing wind accompanied by tongues of fire that come to rest on many persons in the crowd. The crowd itself is a culturally and ethnically mixed group of folks who, under normal circumstances, do not speak the same language or associate freely with one another. Yet, on this morning, they hear one another as though they were hearing what was said in their own languages. Indeed, the whole thing was enough of a spectacle that onlookers thought the disciples and the growing crowd had been drinking too much wine. The trouble with the story of Pentecost may very well be that it is so spectacular. We find ourselves wondering what the whole thing must have looked like. We readily think about and debate the most eccentric aspects of the story. We want to know whether the tongues of fire were visible to the naked eye. We want to know whether the people gathered there that morning could actually feel the wind blowing.

Our fascination with the eccentricities of Pentecost is hardly surprising. We are naturally curious about such extraordinary things. The problem is not so much that we are curious, but that we are often unable to look beyond the more exotic aspects of the story. What happens to us when we encounter the story of Pentecost is not altogether unlike what happens when we encounter a movie with extraordinary special effects. We are so mesmerized and energized by the special effects that we often miss the more subtle and substantial points the movie is trying to make. It is only upon subsequent reflection and conversation with our friends that we realize what the movie was actually about.

For those who have been initiated into various forms of modern skepticism and doubt, the problem is even worse. We do not simply find the rushing wind and tongues of fire fascinating in a way that is analogous to extraordinary special effects in movies. Rather, we find the whole thing highly doubtful, if not downright preposterous. Consequently, we get so sidetracked by inquiries into the metaphysics of the person and work of the Holy Spirit that we miss the theological points that the story wants to make.[27]

If we want to see the more subtle and substantial theological points embedded in the story of Pentecost, then we need temporarily to set aside the more eccentric and exotic aspects of the story. Moving beyond the eccentric and exotic, we need to pay close attention to what happens in the days leading up to Pentecost all the way through the days and weeks that follow. When we do so, the following five features of the story are theologically significant for our understanding of the nature of the church.

(1) If the days following Jesus' crucifixion were filled with doubt and despair, then the days following his resurrection were filled with wonder and deep delight. The disciples witnessed the resurrected Lord with their own eyes, they shared meals with him, and they learned directly from him about the kingdom of God now breaking in upon them. All of this happened for approximately forty days (Acts 1:3). Amid all of the excitement, however, their Lord was once again taken from them, returning to his Father in heaven (Acts 1:9).

With the ascension, the disciples literally lost sight of Jesus. They could no longer hear or see their beloved teacher and Lord. They were, we might say, sheep who could no longer see or hear their shepherd; they were servants who could no longer hear their master. To be sure, they were more confident now than they had been after the crucifixion. Yet the ascension must surely have triggered a measure of anxiety in Jesus' followers.

The truth is that very little is known about the disciples' lives from the time of Jesus' ascension to the day of Pentecost. We do not have diaries or other firsthand accounts of what the disciples were thinking and feeling at this strange time in their journey. Yet what we know is instructive. Having lost sight of their beloved Lord, the disciples held fast to Jesus' promise that his Father would send another to teach them all things and to empower them for mission and witness throughout the world (John 14:26; Acts 1:8). Indeed, the fact that the disciples were doing exactly what Jesus commanded them to do is evidence that they continued to trust Jesus. On the day of Pentecost, they were tarrying together in Jerusalem (Acts 1:4).

We should note something important about the logic of tarrying in this particular case. Initially, we might imagine that the disciples were waiting aimlessly for the next big thing to happen. The truth is that Peter and the others did not pass the time staring absentmindedly at the four walls of the upper room. Rather, Jesus' earliest followers were engaged in a more active form of tarrying or waiting. More specifically, the disciples were keen to do two things during this time of tarrying. On the one hand, they were keen to tarry together in prayer. And while we have no record of the content of their prayers at this time, it is reasonable to assume the disciples were praying in the manner in which Jesus had previously instructed them. After all, the

Lord's Prayer is about inviting God's kingdom to come, which was the very thing Jesus was discussing on the eve of his ascension (Acts 1:3).

On the other hand, the disciples at no point lost sight of the extraordinary event they had just witnessed. Put simply, they could not stop thinking and talking about the resurrection of Jesus. Thus, during this time of tarrying together in prayer, Peter addressed the disciples concerning Judas' fate and the need to replace him. Unfortunately, we tend to get so hung up on questions about whether Judas freely betrayed Jesus or whether Judas is now in heaven that we miss the point of this part of the story entirely. For Peter and the others, it was imperative to replace Judas with someone who could assist them in the work of bearing witness to Jesus' resurrection (Acts 1:15-26).

(2) Another feature of the Pentecost event with which we need to come to grips is the fact that something truly extraordinary happened on the day of Pentecost. We can do this without fixing on the mechanics, say, of speaking in tongues. Indeed, to debate how the tongues of fire worked can be a serious distraction from the real point of the story. The point of the story is that, on the day of Pentecost, something decidedly new took place. Jesus' followers encountered the Holy Spirit in a way that surpassed their indirect encounters with the Holy Spirit in the life of Jesus.[28] There could be no doubt about what was happening. The one whom Jesus promised his Father would send was now here. As a result, things would never be the same. Thus when Peter stood up to speak, he could not help himself, declaring that Joel's prophecy was being fulfilled before their eyes (Acts 2:15-21). The Spirit was now being poured out on all humankind. The kingdom of God was now coming in power. The disciples' encounter with the Holy Spirit was now as tangible and undeniable as their encounter with the resurrected Lord had been a few days earlier.

(3) Yet another crucial feature of the Pentecost event has to do with the way in which Peter understood the significance of the outpouring of the Holy Spirit on all flesh. Once again, we readily focus our attention on peripheral matters, raising questions about whether the special gifts that accompanied the coming of the Spirit on the day of Pentecost continue in the church to this day. To be sure, there is a place and time to discuss such matters, but we need to be careful not to miss what is most significant about the coming of the Holy Spirit *for the disciples*. For Peter and the others, the outpouring of the Holy Spirit

is the ultimate validation of the resurrection and lordship of Jesus. Thus Peter tells the crowd that what they see and hear is the direct result of the resurrection and exaltation of Jesus. The coming of the Spirit should leave no doubt that "God has made Him both Lord and Messiah, this Jesus whom you crucified" (Acts 2:36). Just as the Spirit had borne witness to Jesus throughout his life and ministry, the Spirit was now bearing witness to Jesus on the day of Pentecost.

(4) The fourth significant feature of the Pentecost event concerns what the disciples and the larger crowd began to do in the days and weeks immediately following the outpouring of the Spirit. Initially, they were engaged in the work of repentance and baptism for the forgiveness of sins, but they did not stop there. Following the baptisms of thousands of persons, the earliest followers of Jesus were continually eating together, praying, devoting themselves to the teaching of the apostles, selling their goods in order to share resources, and worshipping God. Thus their life together consisted of both a vertical and a horizontal dimension, the vertical dimension having to do with attentiveness to God and the horizontal dimension having to do with attentiveness to one another and to those around them.

(5) Finally, we need to note that, despite all they had seen and experienced, the earliest followers of Jesus remained an altogether human lot. As both the remainder of the book of Acts and the Pauline and pseudo-Pauline letters make clear, the post-Pentecost church was anything but an ecclesiastical utopia. Serving as a priest or pastor to one of the earliest Christian churches would have been no less challenging than serving as the priest or pastor of a church today. The members of the earliest churches often disagreed with one another, failed to differentiate between the true gospel and false gospels, took one another to court, hoarded their resources, struggled with a lack of courage in the face of persecution, considered returning to Judaism, dabbled in pagan rituals, mismanaged funds, and wrestled with all manner of sin and corruption. Nevertheless, they somehow banded together and, with the help of the Holy Spirit, worshipped the Holy Trinity and bore witness to the life, death, and resurrection of Jesus in word and deed throughout the world. Indeed, when we consider the many failings of the earliest churches, it is exceedingly hard to account for the survival and gradual spread of Christianity in the first

and second centuries apart from the ongoing presence and work of the Holy Spirit.

When we stand back and review the wider narrative of the pentecostal origins of the church, a range of activities are prominent, including tarrying, praying, welcoming and celebrating the Holy Spirit, repenting, baptizing, learning from the apostles, breaking bread together, combining and sharing resources, worshipping together, and, most importantly, bearing witness to Christ crucified, resurrected, and exalted. Whatever else the church may have been or done in the originating womb of Pentecost, these are among the most prominent and pronounced actions and activities. To the extent the church is what the church does, the church is a community given over to waiting upon the Lord in prayer, the reception and celebration of the Holy Spirit, humble repentance and baptism, the study of doctrine, the praise and worship of the Holy Trinity in a spirit of thanksgiving, a deep concern for one another's welfare, and a vital and vibrant witness to Jesus Christ.

We would be remiss, however, if we did not accentuate the presence and power of the Holy Spirit in the origination of the church. Prior to the outpouring of the Holy Spirit, the earliest followers of Jesus were limited to the work of tarrying together in prayer and remembering the resurrection amongst themselves. The point here is not to downplay that work. On the contrary, as we will see in a moment, there is much to be said for tarrying in prayer when the church is struggling through a period of deep fear and anxiety. Yet when the Spirit comes at Pentecost, the Spirit empowers and emboldens the earliest followers of Jesus to repent, to baptize and to catechize new converts, to share their resources with one another, and to bear witness to Jesus with power and effectiveness across the face of the earth. Moreover, through the ongoing presence and work of the Holy Spirit, the church continued faithfully to worship the Holy Trinity and courageously to bear witness to the resurrection of Jesus even as she struggled to overcome her many failings and sins and to be courageous in the face of martyrdom. As NMC puts it,

> Just as in the life of Christ the Holy Spirit was active from the very conception of Jesus through the paschal mystery and remains even now the Spirit of the risen Lord, so also in the life of the Church

the Spirit forms Christ in believers and in their community. The Spirit incorporates human beings into the body of Christ through faith and baptism, enlivens and strengthens them as the body of Christ nourished and sustained in the Lord's Supper, and leads them to the full accomplishment of their vocation.[29]

In the light of the pentecostal origins of the church, we can now venture a preliminary definition of the nature of the church. From its inception, the church has been and is a charismatic community whose life depends entirely on the presence and power of the Holy Spirit, through whom and by whom the church does everything that she does, including proclaiming the good news about the life, death, and resurrection of Jesus; assisting persons in repentance for sin; catechizing and baptizing new converts; praying and worshipping together; freely sharing resources within and without the community; and breaking bread together.[30] All the church is and all the church does in both its vertical and horizontal dimensions is a matter of divine gratuity and generosity. The church receives her life originally and continually from the Holy Spirit who, sent by the Father, enables the church effectively to bear witness to Jesus Christ and to be incorporated into his body in every aspect of her life.

The Church as Icon of the Trinity

One of the advantages of thinking about the nature of the church in light of the pentecostal origins of the church is that doing so allows us to reappropriate the descriptions of the church in the Nicene Creed, in Protestant confessions of faith, and in the New Testament in a way that does not lead either to denial of or despair over the church's collective sins and failures. Indeed, understanding the nature of the church in light of the church's pentecostal origins puts these descriptions of the church into proper theological perspective in at least two very important ways.

First and foremost, understanding the nature of the church in light of the church's pentecostal origins enables us truly to attribute holiness, unity, catholicity, and apostolicity to the church. Similarly, it enables us rightly to attribute to the church the exemplary qualities suggested by the New Testament metaphors for the church. We can do these things because Pentecost reminds us that the church came into existence originally and has existed continuously ever since because the Spirit is present in and to the church. As Irenaeus put it, "Where the Church is, there is also the Spirit of God and where the Spirit of God is, there are also the Church and all grace."[31]

We can attribute to the church then and now all that the descriptions of the church in the Nicene Creed, in the Protestant confessions, and in the New Testament signify precisely because *the Holy Trinity is present in and to the church.* For example, we can rightly say that the church is holy because the Holy Trinity present in and to the church is holy. Likewise, if the pure word of God is proclaimed and the sacraments duly administered, then it is not because the priest or the pastor is homiletically sound or because he or she flawlessly pronounces the words over the Eucharist. Rather, the pure word of God is preached and the sacraments duly administered in the church precisely because the Holy Spirit is present and at work in the church's liturgical services, bearing witness to Jesus Christ crucified, resurrected, and exalted over all the earth. In saying these things, we do not intend to minimize the importance of homiletics or due care in the administration of the sacraments. Rather, we are simply observing that it is ultimately the Holy Spirit's presence that transforms our feeble attempts at proclamation into the pure word of God, and that it is Holy Spirit who enables us to discern the real presence of Jesus Christ in the Eucharist and to be transformed by it.

In this sense, the descriptions of the church in the Creed, in Protestant confessions, and in the New Testament can rightly be applied to the church regardless of whether they can be applied directly to the clergy and laity who make up the churches. For example, despite the visible disunity of the church throughout the world, we can rightly attribute unity to the church insofar as it is the same Holy Spirit who enables the church in all of its manifestations to bear witness to Jesus Christ and to worship the Holy Trinity in truth and love. Even more profoundly, we can attribute unity to the church insofar as the Holy Spirit who animates the churches throughout the world is ever drawing them into the fullness of the unity of the Holy Trinity, whom the church worships in joyous thanksgiving and praise.

To see this clearly, we need only to recall that, on the working definition of the church given above, everything the church is and everything the church has she is and has *derivatively.* Alternatively, the church has nothing that she has not received, and she is nothing apart from the continual presence and power of the Holy Spirit and therefore of the Holy Trinity in and to her life. We can apply all that the Creed, the confessions, and the New Testament says about the church to the church precisely because the Holy Trinity is present in and to the church in her worship, her sacraments, her prayers, her proclamation, and in every other aspect of her life. As *NMC* says,

> The Church is not merely the sum of individual believers in communion with God, nor primarily the mutual communion of individual believers among themselves. It is their common partaking in the life of God (2 Pet 1:4), who as Trinity is the source and focus of all communion. Thus the Church is *both a divine and a human reality*.[32]

This really is a momentous statement about the nature of the church. It is momentous because it helps to correct our thinking about what it means to say that the church is a communion or fellowship (*koinonia*). All too often, when we use the language of communion or fellowship, we have in mind relationships among believers. Thus we routinely refer to the "fellowship of believers" or the "communion of saints." To be sure, the church is a fellowship of believers and a communion of saints, but the church is also more than that. Thus when the Apostle Paul uses the word *koinonia*, he has in mind not merely a fellowship of believers but "the communion of the Holy Spirit" (2 Cor 13:13). In other words, "the source and focus of all communion" is not ourselves; *it is the Holy Trinity*. Indeed, we have genuine communion with one another when our communion with one another only is grounded in and revolves around our communion with the Holy Trinity. To put the matter somewhat differently, we have genuine communion with one another only because we are being incorporated into the Trinitarian life of God.

When we understand the church as a fellowship or communion this way, there are important implications for how we think about the nature of the church. At least one theologian has attempted to capture these implications by describing the church as an "icon of the Holy Trinity."[33] And while there may be some limitations to this way of describing the nature of the church,[34] there is also at least one major advantage. The notion that the church is an icon of the Holy Trinity reminds us that, in and through the sacramental life of the church, the Holy Trinity really is present to the world—that in and through the church the Holy Spirit is ever at work redeeming the creation and incorporating it into the Trinitarian life of God.

A second consideration is in the immediate vicinity. Given the presence of the Holy Spirit and therefore of the Holy Trinity in and to the life of the church, surely there is a sense in which we can truly apply what is said of the church in the Creed, confessions, and New Testament not only to God but also to the church's members. We can do so because the presence of the Holy Trinity in and to the church sanctifies us, making us one, holy, catholic, and apostolic, enabling us to preach the pure word of God and duly to administer the sacraments, and making us a city on a hill, a light to the nations, the spotless bride of Christ, and the branches of the true vine. We can apply all that is said of the church not only to God but also to the church's members because the Holy Spirit enables us to mirror the same image of God mirrored with exactness by Jesus Christ, to whom the Spirit is ever and always bearing witness in the church. Put simply, the church's members share in the unity and holiness of the Trinity who is ever present and at work in every aspect of her life (John 17).

What we need here is a way to take seriously two realities which, on the surface, appear to be mutually exclusive. On the one hand, we have the undeniable reality of the many sins and failings of the churches across the centuries. We have the reality of disunity, a lack of holiness, a lack of apostolicity and catholicity, and so on. On the other hand, we have the reality that is the originating and ongoing presence and work of the Holy Spirit and therefore of the Holy Trinity in and through the sacramental life of the church on behalf of the world.

We can reconcile these conflicting realities by recalling that the coming of the Holy Spirit at Pentecost was not to establish the church for the church's sake. Rather, the Spirit establishes the church as the primary means of witness to the kingdom of God here and now. Thus the church is intimately related to the rule and reign of God in history, but the church is not simply to be equated with the kingdom of God. At her best, the church bears witness in her life to what the kingdom of God will be like when it comes in fullness. The church is among the first fruits of the kingdom of God, but the kingdom of God is itself an eschatological reality whose complete fulfillment yet lies in the future. Thus *NMC* is exactly right when it says,

> The Church is *an eschatological reality*, already anticipating the Kingdom. However, the Church on earth is not yet the full visible realization of the Kingdom. Being also an historical reality, it is exposed to the ambiguities of all human history and therefore needs constant repentance and renewal in order to respond fully to its vocation.[35]

Because the rule and reign of God to which the church bears witness in her life is not yet fully realized, the church struggles fully to embody what is ascribed to her in the Creed, in Protestant confessions of faith, and in the New Testament. Otherwise put, what is ascribed to the church in these sources is, like the kingdom of God itself, an eschatological reality to which the church bears witness and toward which the church lives and strains, however imperfectly. Thus it is entirely fitting that the marks of the church in the Nicene Creed are situated between the confession of faith in the Holy Spirit and the eschatological confession with which the Creed concludes.

Unfortunately, putting the descriptions of the church into their proper eschatological context actually gives rise to a third danger. In addition to denial and despair, the church that emphasizes the eschatological nature of its life will be tempted to *resignation*. To say that the marks of the church are eschatological is to invite people to underestimate the extent to which the Holy Spirit sanctifies the church here and now, truly making her one, holy, catholic, and apostolic. We will be tempted to interpret the eschatological nature of the marks of the church in a way that makes confession, true repentance, and the genuine quest for unity, holiness, catholicity, and apostolicity unnecessary. We will come to accept disunity, a lack of holiness and catholicity, and infidelity to apostolic teaching as simply the given features of our eschatological situation. To expect more would be tantamount to expecting the impossible.[36]

At this crucial juncture, we must ask ourselves whether or not we believe in the transforming and sanctifying work of the Holy Spirit. To sidestep this matter is functionally to embrace a doctrine of the Holy Spirit in which the Spirit is not a Spirit of power but an impotent Spirit incapable of doing anything truly to restore us to newness of life;

to knit us together in one body that is holy, catholic, and apostolic; to enable us to proclaim the pure word of God and to administer the sacraments rightly; and to incorporate us into the Trinitarian life of God. Either we will believe the Holy Spirit is a Spirit of life and power and of all unity and holiness, or we will live as though the Spirit is incapable of making a real difference in our lives. Either we will seek the Spirit in true repentance and humble expectation, or we will ignore to our own peril the very source of our ongoing life together.

If the churches that we know and love fall short of all that is ascribed to the church in the Nicene Creed, in Protestant confessions and articles, and in the New Testament, this may say more about their need for renewal than about the Spirit's ability to sanctify and to immerse the church in the fullness of the Trinitarian life of God.[37] Indeed, as we will see in chapter 3 up ahead, the renewal the church needs most is precisely a renewal in oneness, holiness, apostolicity, and catholicity. For now, we need to explore the significance of our theological reflections on the nature of the church for our anxiety, for our thinking about the various visions for renewal that prophetic leaders and movements are offering the church today, and for our need to navigate the tensions than can emerge between those visions and ecclesial structures.

The Nature of the Church and the Quest for Renewal

At the outset of this chapter, we observed that, when we do not begin our reflections on the church with the nature of the church, we perpetually run into two problems. First, we tend to develop visions of the mission of the church and then proceed to fall into despair when we cannot meet the demands of those visions by the sheer force of our collective will. Second, we have a tendency to forget that our best resources are neither the ones that we invent nor the ones that we purchase, but the resources that we receive from the Holy Spirit, the most important of which is the presence of the Holy Spirit among us.

Even when we have spent considerable time thinking about the nature of the church, the two foregoing tendencies have a way of getting the best of us. This is especially true in an age of fear and anxiety. For example, our tendency to go straight for the mission of the church can cause us to skip past the deep insights that have surfaced in our thinking on the nature of the church. We quickly discern in the pentecostal origins of the church a vision for the *mission* of the church. We tell ourselves that, to fix the church today, we need simply to set about *doing* all the things that we see the church doing immediately before, during, and after Pentecost. In other words, in an age of anxiety, we want above all else to take action. We want to take control of the situation by putting together and implementing a plan. To be sure, a plan that calls the church to imitate the church in and around Pentecost would not strike many Christians as particularly objectionable. However, if such a plan is not carefully located within a wider vision of the nature of the church, then it will be just as likely to result in despair or denial as any other plan that we might hatch to save the church.

Similarly, fear and anxiety often cause us to put our faith and hope in resources other than the Holy Spirit. For example, many clergy and church leaders are currently looking to prophetic leaders and movements to save the church. We see in the missional church or the emerging church nothing less than our salvation. We tell ourselves that, if we would only become more purpose-driven, then we would see the kind of dramatic turnaround that we are longing for. Thus we devote ourselves to a favored prophetic leader or movement. We attend their conferences, buy their books, and bookmark their blogs. We pull out all the stops to adopt and to implement their visions for mission and ministry. We may even go so far as to integrate the name of the movement into the name of our local church. Thus we become "Grace United Methodist Church . . . an emerging community."[38]

As we said in the introduction, prophetic leaders and movements can be and often are gifts of the Holy Spirit in and through which the Spirit works to correct the church as she goes on her way. Yet they are not themselves the Holy Spirit. In and of themselves, they do not have the power to breathe new life into the church. This does not mean that we should not listen carefully and prayerfully to what they have to say or, better yet, to what the Spirit may be saying to the churches *through* them. It simply means that we must be on guard against our tendency to forget that the ultimate resource for church renewal is the presence and power of the Holy Spirit in our midst.

At the other extreme, fear and anxiety can cause us to eschew and to dismiss the prophetic in favor of clinging for all we are worth to ecclesial structures. Thus many clergy and church leaders insist that, if we will simply recommit ourselves to the system, then the system will save us. For example, when fear and anxiety take hold, United Methodist Church dignitaries invariably begin talking about renewing the "connection." Connection or connectionalism is simply an umbrella term for the various structures around which the Methodist system revolves, e.g., annual and general conferences, *The Book of Discipline*, the appointment system, and the like. Unfortunately, when we listen closely, our talk about renewing the connection often boils down to an urging of Methodist clergy and lay leaders to be more committed to the structures that make up the system. In short, we are really saying, "If we will only work a little harder, the system will save us."[39]

As we noted in the introduction, ecclesial structures are gifts of the Holy Spirit in and through which the Spirit works to incorporate us into the Trinitarian life of God.[40] Yet ecclesial structures are not themselves the Holy Spirit. In and of themselves, they do not have the power to breathe new life into the church. This does not mean that the Spirit cannot work through ecclesial structures to renew the church. Rather, it simply means that we need to be on guard against our tendency to forget that the ultimate resource for renewal is not our structures, but the presence and power of the Holy Spirit in our midst.

If we are to overcome our tendency to put our trust in our own resources (whether they be prophetic or structural), then we must focus our minds and hearts on the nature of the church before we set out to think about or to work for renewal. Before we take any actions, devise any plans, or buy into any program (whether old or new), we need to take time to recall not simply *what* we are but *whose* we are. We need to remember that we are a charismatic community brought into being and sustained each day by the presence and power of the Holy Spirit. We need to remember that we have nothing that we have not received. We need to remember that the Holy Spirit is ever present among us, incorporating us into the Trinitarian life of God.

The insight that we most need to take away from our account of the pentecostal origins of the church is one that is both simple and profound. When the earliest followers of Jesus literally lost sight of their Lord, they did not rush to attend a seminar on what to do next. Nor did they cling for all their worth to the time-tested structures of Judaism. To be sure, the disciples later organized themselves and set out to spread the gospel throughout the known world, but they did not do this initially. Initially, they did one thing. They tarried together in prayer.

In many ways, the church in the postmodern West faces a similar situation. We have, metaphorically speaking, lost sight of our Lord. We are anxious and afraid. We are deeply concerned about the present state and future of our churches. Yet, if we take seriously the notion that the church is a charismatic community whose life depends entirely on the presence and work of the Holy Spirit, then it follows immediately that the best way to deal with our anxiety is to call upon the Holy Spirit in prayer. Indeed, we ought to regard with suspicion any and all proposals for renewal that turn initially to anything or anyone other than the Holy Spirit for direction. To be sure, the Holy Spirit works through prophetic leaders and movements as well as through ecclesial structures to breathe new life into the church. Nevertheless, all efforts at renewal should begin with the recognition that it is the Spirit who brought the church to life in the beginning and it is the Spirit who will rescue us when we are in trouble.

Once we recognize that the Holy Spirit is our only source and hope for church renewal, the first step in the quest for renewal is plain to see. Before we turn to prophetic leaders and movements or to existing structures for help, we need to commit ourselves to the hard work of tarrying together in prayer. To be sure, the suggestion that we should begin our quest for renewal by tarrying together in prayer will strike some as hopelessly mundane. Surely the importance of prayer is obvious to even the conventionally pious. Surely this is tantamount to saying we ought to put gas in the car before we set out on a trip. Yet it is precisely the widespread sense that prayer is a given that should give us pause. In many quarters today, it is not altogether clear that the church knows the difference between tarrying together in prayer and loitering together at a church bake sale. In the worst cases, one gets the impression that prayer is an obligatory preface to the real work that needs to be done. There is almost a palpable expectation that prayers be kept short so that we can get on with more important things.

The work of tarrying together in prayer is not something to be taken lightly. As Sarah Coakley says, the "faithful presence [of prayer] can be nothing short of electric."[41] Indeed, to tarry together in prayer is to admit that we are out of answers, that we have lost confidence in the ability of marketing schemes, new technology, and fund-raising campaigns to save us. It is to turn our attention heavenward and to ask God the Father once again to pour out the Spirit promised by the Son. In this sense, tarrying together in prayer really is simple work. We need only to invoke the Holy Spirit to come to our aid and then to wait attentively for the Holy Spirit to do so.[42]

Here then is the first vital step toward church renewal in the light of our working definition of the nature of the church. The church that truly yearns for renewal will commit herself to one thing above all else. She will invite the Holy Spirit to come, and she will do so continuously until the Spirit shows up. She will do so at the outset of every worship service, staff meeting, educational offering, and in every other phase of her life. Her constant prayer will be "Come, Holy Spirit." Her life will be one continuous *epiclesis*. She may even want to schedule special weeknight prayer vigils in which prayers are limited to invoking the Holy Spirit to come, to the confession of sin, and to the expression of a ready willingness to cede all power and control to the Holy Spirit. Of course, we cannot know in advance when or how the Spirit will respond. All we can know is that, when the Spirit does respond, it is likely to be unmistakable for anything else. It may even be accompanied by things eccentric and exotic.

Finally, inviting the Holy Spirit to come and to renew the church is the easy part. Anyone can do this. The hard part is waiting. Waiting is not something persons living in the postmodern West like to do. Indeed, to live in the postmodern West is to take charge of our lives, to take action, to take ownership and responsibility, and to get on with things. We pride ourselves on being independent and self-sufficient, on not having to wait on anyone or anything—including God—to get the job done. We reside in a land of plenty, and we have come to trust above all in our own resources and our own resourcefulness. We so readily and easily forget that we have nothing that we have not received. Most of all, however, we forget that our resolve to be in control has devastating consequences. As Richard John Neuhaus once put it, "It is our determination to be independent by being in control that makes us unavailable to God."[43]

Beginning the quest for renewal by reflecting theologically on the nature of the church has reminded us that the church is a charismatic community that is entirely dependent on the Holy Spirit for all she is and for all she has. Apart from prolonged reflection on the nature of the church, we will continue *to look to* prophetic leaders and movements or to existing church structures for our salvation. By contrast, if in the light of our reflections on the nature of the church we will commit ourselves to the work of tarrying together in prayer, then we will prepare the way for the Holy Spirit *to work through* prophetic leaders and movements and through ecclesial structures to make us one, holy, catholic, and apostolic; to enable us to proclaim the pure word of God and rightly to administer the sacraments; and to make us a light to the nations, a city on a hill, the branches of the true vine, and the spotless bride of Christ. Even so, come Holy Spirit.

Chapter 2

The Mission of the Church

We began thinking theologically about church renewal by inquiring after the *nature* of the church. After identifying the marks of the church in the Nicene Creed and Protestant confessions, as well as some of the metaphors for the church in the New Testament, we grounded our vision of the nature of the church in the events that transpired at Pentecost, which is to say, in pneumatology and eschatology. We concluded that the church is above all a charismatic community whose life depends entirely on the presence and power of the Holy Spirit. On the basis of this vision of the nature of the church, we stressed the importance of tarrying together in prayer as the first step on the journey to renewal.

In this chapter, we turn to a second fundamental issue in ecclesiology, namely, the *mission* of the church. We want to know why the Holy Spirit breathed life into the church at Pentecost in the first place, and we want to know why the Spirit continues to breathe life into the church today. In our reflections on the nature of the church we have already gained some initial insights into the church's mission. We should not be surprised by this, insofar as the mission of the church is intimately related to the church's nature. Thus we have already noted that the Holy Spirit works in and through the church *to incorporate us into the Trinitarian life of God.* In other words, the Spirit works in and through the church to bring us into communion with God the Father through Jesus Christ, the eternally begotten Son. We must now develop these insights more fully. Before we do, we need to take a moment to observe some potential problems with the language and logic of mission.

The Language and Logic of Mission

In setting out to think about the mission of the church, two temptations surface almost immediately. First, we instinctively want to limit the church's mission to one thing. We reason that the church must have one and only one overriding mission in the world. If the church has more than one mission, then we will almost certainly become divided over how best to spend our time and resources. If the church is to be efficient and focused in her work, then the church is going to need singleness of heart and mind. Let us call this the *criterion of simplicity*.

The problem with this approach to thinking about the mission of the church is easy to see. The moment we designate one thing that purportedly constitutes the church's mission, someone will make life difficult for us by pointing out other things for which an equally strong case might be made. For example, suppose we insist that the church exists to make disciples of Jesus Christ. Initially, this is quite attractive. After all, making disciples is at the heart of the Great Commission. But just as we are ready to insist that the church's only mission is to make disciples, someone will rain on our parade by insisting that the church's real mission is to worship God. If we attempt to combine worship and making disciples, someone else will argue that the church ultimately exists to care for the orphan and the widow in her midst. And yet another person will insist that the church's mission is to care for the whole of creation.

At this stage, a second temptation readily and naturally surfaces. Having set out to identify the church's one overriding mission in the world, we will be tempted to list anything and everything that comes to mind, claiming all of it as the church's mission. After all, each one of the foregoing suggestions is defensible on the basis of Scripture and the Christian tradition. Thus we will be tempted to swing from one extreme to the other, abandoning simplicity and singularity of heart and mind for plurality of purpose. We will reason that the church is not simply to make disciples or to worship; she is also to preach, to teach, to baptize, to administer the sacraments, to provide assistance to the poor, to work for social justice, to care for the earth, and the like. Let us call this the *criterion of comprehensiveness*.

If the first approach is too narrow, then the second approach is too broad. The danger here is a loss of focus. Before we know it, the church becomes the sort of organization that does a million things poorly. We have no orienting concern on the basis of which we make all subsequent decisions. We have no clear understanding of mission on the basis of which we identify and deploy resources for ministry. The end result is predictable. Laity and clergy wear themselves out trying to do too many things. We lack any sense of cohesiveness and direction. We forget what or who it was that brought us together in the first place.

For those of us who live in the postmodern West, the second approach to thinking about the church's mission is particularly problematic. Plagued by fear and anxiety about the future of the church, we instinctively want to seize control of the situation. We believe that there are no problems that we cannot fix ourselves. Thus, when faced with church decay and decline, we launch fund-raising campaigns; we preach on the importance of tithing; we update the technology; we change the worship; we rearrange the furniture; we wear name badges for the visitors; we relocate; we hire staff; we abandon Sunday School; we begin new outreach programs; we reemphasize the need to serve the poor in our communities; and on and on it goes. We proceed as though there is nothing wrong that money and some old-fashioned effort cannot fix. We forget that the church is a charismatic community whose life is utterly dependent on the presence and power of the Holy Spirit.

Any approach to the church's mission that emphasizes comprehensiveness will constantly run the risk of playing into the Western dogma that we can save ourselves and our institutions simply by working harder, by putting in more hours, by being more committed, and the like. Indeed, the belief that we can save ourselves is so foundational in both the modern and postmodern West that it is like a rule that we obey so habitually in our thinking that we are not even aware of it. As Ludwig Wittgenstein, an influential twentieth-century philosopher, once said, we "do not choose" to obey such a rule; we "obey it *blindly*."[1] In other words, we have followed the rule that we can save ourselves for so long that it governs all of our thoughts and actions.

When we look a little more closely, the belief that we can save ourselves through hard work is hiding behind a great deal of our thinking and discoursing about the mission of the church and about church renewal.[2] For example, when we declare that the mission of the church is to worship God or to do evangelism or to save souls, we are obeying the rule in our thinking that salvation is something that we do. We remain the primary, if not the sole, agents. *We* are carrying out the mission of the church by worshiping God. *We* are fulfilling the church's mission by doing the work of evangelism or by advocating for social justice. The same thing holds for church renewal. *We* are raising money. *We* are updating the worship. *We* are hiring staff. *We* are relocating.

We can now see a more subtle reason for the immense popularity of mission statements over the last twenty-five years. We tell ourselves that we adopt mission statements because they help to bring focus to our life and work. If I am right, however, we also adopt mission statements because the very language of mission appeals to our belief in our ability to save ourselves. Indeed, few things are more appealing to the Western mind than the idea that we have a mission to accomplish, a job to do, a goal to meet, a problem to solve.

We should note carefully that the language of mission is not in and of itself the problem. The problem is the way that the Western mind so readily absorbs the language of mission into a deeply held system of beliefs and values, all of which serve to undergird the overriding Western myth of self-sufficiency. Of course, this absorption is not limited to our talk about mission statements. Rather, any and all talk of mission is subject to the rules that govern the Western mind. In other words, the same process of absorption can just as easily happen when we talk more generally about the mission of the church.

If we are to overcome this problem, then we need constantly to remind ourselves that the church has nothing that she has not received, including her mission. We must remind ourselves that it is ultimately the Holy Trinity, and not the church per se, who has a mission.[3] The church is simply blessed to be part of the Holy Trinity's mission in and to the world. As Jürgen Moltmann puts it,

In the movements of the Trinitarian history of God's dealings with the world the church finds and discovers itself, in all the relationships which comprehend its life. It finds itself on the path traced by this history of God's dealings with the world, and it discovers itself as one element in the movements of the divine sending, gathering together and experience. It is not the church that has a mission of salvation to fulfill in the world; it is the mission of the Son and the Spirit through the Father that includes the church, creating a church as it goes on its way.[4]

NMC agrees, making it clear that, rather than having its own mission, the church "participates in the mission of Christ."[5] Moreover, it is not the church that saves, but God who "restores and enriches communion with humanity, granting eternal life in God's Triune Being." For her part, the church "must witness to and participate in God's reconciliation, healing, and transformation of creation."[6]

To insist that the church does not so much *have* a mission as she does an opportunity to *participate* in God's mission is one thing. To recall this distinction each and every day is another thing altogether. Apart from such intentional recollection, we will succumb perpetually to the rules that govern the mind of the West. Grabbing our bootstraps, focusing our minds, and gritting our teeth, we will attempt to bring about church renewal by the sheer force of our collective will. In the process, all of our talk about the mission of the church will actually become the very mechanism by which we, albeit unwittingly, reinforce the myth of our self-sufficiency.[7]

We can now see more clearly why tarrying together in prayer is the first step on the path to renewal. The church that tarries together in prayer will be less likely to forget that the source of her life and the hope for her renewal is none other than the Holy Spirit. The church that invokes the Holy Spirit at the outset of every worship service, of every staff meeting, indeed of everything that she undertakes to do will, over time, learn to see the myth of self-sufficiency for what it really is, namely, a lie that prevents us from turning to and desiring God.

At this stage, someone might observe that prayer can just as easily play into the myth of self-sufficiency. In other words, someone might suggest that we can approach prayer as yet one more thing that *we* do. We can understand and appreciate this concern, but it is ill-founded.

Rightly understood, prayer is something that the Holy Spirit does in and through us, not something that we do by and for ourselves. To be sure, we cooperate with the Holy Spirit and are thereby active agents in the work of prayer, but the Holy Spirit is nonetheless the primary causal agent, the one who initiates all true prayer.[8] As Karl Barth once put it, "Prayer is a grace, an offer of God."[9]

Assuming that we are now pursuing church renewal from a disposition of fervent prayer, the next step is to reflect theologically on the mission of the church in a way that works deliberately to avoid reinforcing the myth of self-sufficiency. Far from contradicting or competing with the work of tarrying together in prayer, such reflection complements this work in a logical and natural way. If we are to begin our quest for renewal by invoking the Holy Spirit, then it is logical and natural to want to know more about the One to whom we are turning for help.

A good way to learn about someone is to pay close attention to what he or she does. In this case, if we want to know more about the One whom we are calling and waiting upon in prayer, then we need to pay attention to what the Holy Spirit has done in the life of the church from the beginning down through the centuries. We need to know what activities, in addition to prayer, are most characteristic of the Holy Spirit. We also need to identify the resources the Holy Spirit has given to the church for carrying out the work of ministry.[10]

By discerning the characteristic activities of the Holy Spirit in and through the life of the church at Pentecost and across the centuries, we will know better both how to pray and what to expect. Indeed, coming to grips with what the Spirit has done in and through the church across the centuries will help us to differentiate authentic from inauthentic responses to our prayers. To be sure, we want to remain open to anything and everything that the Holy Spirit might want to do in our midst. At the same time, to ignore what the Spirit has done in and through the church across space and time is to raise the likelihood that we will mistake our own schemes and desires for the presence and work of the Holy Spirit.

What follows, then, is a constructive vision of the mission of the church that is grounded in the work of the Holy Spirit. The attentive reader will notice that, on this vision, the church's mission is twofold. As such, it meets the demands of the criteria that we identified above. On the one hand, the vision that follows meets the criterion of simplicity insofar as we are limiting the mission of the church to two things. On the other hand, it meets the criterion of comprehensiveness insofar as the two things that we will identify account for the overwhelming majority of the activities that tend to show up in our thinking about the church's mission and in the mission statements of local congregations.

The Twofold Mission of the Church

Beginning at Pentecost and continuing across the centuries to the present day, we can observe the Holy Spirit enabling and empowering the church to do two things. On the one hand, the Holy Spirit is ever at work in the church, enabling her to worship God. With the help of the Holy Spirit, the church acknowledges and celebrates the rule and reign of God over all of creation in a spirit of humility, joy, and thanksgiving.[11] Thus NMC says, "The Church is called to manifest God's mercy to humanity, and to bring humanity to its purpose—to praise and glorify God together with all the heavenly hosts."[12]

On the other hand, the Holy Spirit is ever at work in the church, enabling her to bear witness to the life, death, and resurrection of Jesus Christ. With the help of the Holy Spirit, the church witnesses to Jesus Christ in *word* and in *deed*. NMC puts it this way:

> As persons who acknowledge Jesus Christ as Lord and Saviour, Christians are called to proclaim the Gospel in word and deed. They are to address those who have not heard, as well as those who are no longer living according to the Gospel, the Good News of the reign of God. They are called to live its values and to be a foretaste of that reign in the world.[13]

Like the church's worship, the church's witness in word and deed consists of an entire range of activities through which the church proclaims and embodies the good news concerning Jesus Christ in a spirit of humility, joy, and thanksgiving.[14]

Before we examine the two aspects of the church's witness more closely, three preliminary observations are in order. First, we need to observe that it is the presence and power of the Holy Spirit at work in her members that enables the church to say and to do all that she says and does in worshipping God and in bearing witness to Jesus Christ.[15]

Apart from the presence and power of the Holy Spirit, the church's worship will be misguided and her witness ineffectual. Consequently, the church needs constantly to invoke the Holy Spirit in every aspect of her life. In planning for worship and in sermon preparation, clergy and laity alike should ask the Holy Spirit to come and to help them keep the focus of worship where it belongs, namely, on the mystery and majesty of God. Similarly, at the outset of every worship service, we should acknowledge the presence of the Holy Spirit among us and invite the Holy Spirit to focus our hearts and minds on the task at hand, eliminating illegitimate worries and distractions. The same holds for bearing witness to Jesus Christ in word and deed. Every time the church bears witness to Jesus Christ in word and deed, her members should begin by acknowledging the presence of the Holy Spirit and asking the Holy Spirit for courage, for a spirit of discernment, for proper humility, and for all grace.

Second, we need to observe that, on this view of the mission of the church, the renewal we seek is precisely the renewal of the church's worship and witness. When we invite the Holy Spirit to come in new and fresh ways, we are asking the Spirit to refocus our worship on God and to enable us more effectively to bear witness to Jesus Christ in word and deed. We are not asking the Holy Spirit to improve our self-esteem, to increase our membership, to grow the youth group, or to bring us wealth, prosperity, and social status. These things may or may not happen in the process. What we are asking for and what we so desperately need is for the Holy Spirit to help us to cease being distracted in worship by ephemeral things, focusing our minds and hearts on the celebration and praise of God. Similarly, we are asking the Holy Spirit to come and to renew our courage for bearing witness to Jesus Christ in word and deed throughout the world.

Third, we need to observe that reflecting theologically on the church's twofold mission takes us beyond ecclesiology proper to other crucial areas of theology. On the one hand, reflecting on the church's worship takes us into the territory of the doctrine of the Trinity. On the other hand, reflecting on the church's witness takes us into the terrain of Christology. With these preliminary observations in place, we are now ready to examine the church's mission in worship and witness more closely.

Worshipping the Holy Trinity

At first glance, we might think that there is no need to explain what we mean by worship. Surely worship is a concept so basic that it is almost self-explanatory. Like farming or fishing, we know worship when we see it.

When we look more closely, however, we notice that Christians often disagree with one another over what constitutes worship, what is acceptable in worship, and the like. For example, many things that Eastern Orthodox Christians regard as acceptable, if not normative, for Christian worship would be anathema to many Southern Baptist Christians, including the veneration of the saints, the use of iconography and incense, and the use of a set or prescribed liturgy. We can also see differences among Christians within the same denomination concerning what is acceptable or normative for worship. A good example of this is the widespread disagreement among United Methodists concerning whether or not nonbaptized persons should be allowed to receive Holy Communion. Similarly, not a few denominations are divided over whether to use the lectionary as a guide for worship.

We could easily think of many more examples of differences and disagreements over what constitutes worship or what is acceptable in worship. However, we would be remiss if we did not highlight one area of deep disagreement that, in recent years, has been particularly problematic among Protestant clergy and congregations, namely, what to make of the phenomenon known as "contemporary worship." To be sure, not all denominations and local congregations have had to wrestle with contemporary worship. Those who have know only too well that few things have divided churches as quickly as the suggestion that a church should consider making its worship more "contemporary." When local congregations have attempted to work around differences of opinion by having two services (one "traditional" and one "contemporary"), they have often found themselves faced with a different set of problems and complaints. Suffice it to say, most pastors who have experimented with "contemporary worship" services in "traditional churches" have more than a few scars to show for their efforts.

At this stage, we should take a moment to spell out what we have in mind when we are talking about contemporizing worship. Generally speaking, efforts to contemporize worship involve three things. First, they involve creating a more relaxed or comfortable ethos for worship. Thus contemporary churches encourage people to dress casually, to help themselves to food and drinks before worship, and to participate only to the degree and in the manner that is comfortable to them. People are free to stand or sit, to take communion or not to take communion, to pray or not to pray. Worship leaders insist that people come as they are and that they act naturally. In some cases, worshippers are told to behave just as they would in their homes. They are literally to make themselves at home.

Second, efforts to contemporize worship often entail minimizing the use of specific theological language. Advocates for contemporary worship encourage worship leaders only to use words nonbelievers can readily understand and to avoid language unique to Christianity or Christian theology. Thus contemporary worship leaders tend to refer generically to God rather than to the Holy Trinity, to address problems or mistakes rather than sin, and to talk in vague terms about becoming better persons rather than deploying the full lexicon of terminology related to salvation, including justification, regeneration, forgiveness, atonement, ransom, liberation, sanctification, perfection, and the like. Moreover, liturgical formulae such as the *Trisagion* and the *Epiclesis* are now regarded as hopelessly out of date.

Third, efforts to contemporize worship usually involve the incorporation of new technology, most notably digital media. Here the goal is to make worship seem familiar by incorporating video clips from well-known movies and television shows, by using popular music, and so on. Implicit in all of this is a belief that, in a digital age, the humble and earthy symbols of Christian worship are out of date, if not downright boring. To keep people's attention, worship must be loud, constantly moving, and full of the digital sounds and images so pervasive in popular culture. Alternatively, the simple eucharistic elements of bread and wine are no match for the special effects of *The Matrix* or for the music of U2. If we are going to offer the Eucharist, then we will need to surround it with something more exciting and eye-catching than a common loaf and a common cup.

It would be difficult to exaggerate the extent to which these changes have led to consternation and even division in local congregations and across entire denominations. Thus differences and disagreements over contemporary worship quickly disintegrate into name calling and casting blame. On the one hand, people who favor "traditional" worship refer to contemporary worship as "irreverent" and "shallow." They insist that, if the church is dying, then it is because the culture has lost the ability to dress nicely, to be respectful in sacred places, and the like. Contemporary worship simply brings a lazy, thoroughly "dumbed-down" and self-absorbed culture into the Holy of Holies.[16] It is nothing less than an act of defilement.

On the other hand, people who favor contemporary worship routinely refer to people who prefer traditional worship as "stuck in the 1950s," "close-minded," and "hostile to change." They insist that, if the church is declining, then it is because "traditionalists" refuse to keep up with the times, to be hospitable to people who do not know all of their favorite hymns, and so on. Advocates of traditional worship are actually the ones who are lazy and self-absorbed, refusing to follow the wind of the Spirit wherever it leads!

As hostile and divisive as the disputes over contemporary worship can be, contemporary worship is not the only front in the worship wars that are currently ravaging many congregations and denominations. In fact, contemporary worship is increasingly an old front in a much larger battle over the church's worship. To be sure, not a few congregations are still fighting battles over contemporary worship, but other battles are now beginning to show up at an alarming rate. One of the more recent battles—the battle over emerging worship—is in some quarters equally, if not more, divisive than contemporary worship.[17]

In many ways, emerging worship is a response to two of the chief criticisms of contemporary worship over the last decade or so. First, critics of contemporary worship often argue that the jettisoning of theological and technical language means that contemporary worship is theologically shallow. The problem with this, according to the critics, is that people are not being formed deeply in the faith. Second, critics of contemporary worship often observe that, when combined with the jettisoning of theological and technical language, the turn to digital media in worship means that there are fewer and fewer discernible differences between the church's worship and life outside of worship. The music in worship is not discernibly different than secular music. Similarly, the PowerPoint presentation accompanying the service resembles all too closely the corporate boardrooms in which so many people are stuck during the week.

In response to these criticisms, architects of emerging worship are seeking to recover more traditional theological language and to create a worship ethos that is noticeably different from secular concerts and corporate boardrooms. Thus, while they still encourage casual dress, they are dialing back on the use of technology, and they are replacing high-voltage spotlights with the dim light of candles. They are also developing more theologically sophisticated music, and they are working to recover lost liturgical practices from the ancient church, including the liturgical calendar, prayers of repentance, the stations of the cross, and the like. Many emerging churches are emphasizing natural symbols and images over all things digital. They are using wood panel icons, a common wood or clay cup for communion, and ashes to make the sign of the cross on their foreheads during Ash Wednesday services.

The backlash against emerging worship is hardly surprising. In the turn to symbols, to "ritual," and to ancient liturgical practices, some critics see a turn to something else altogether, namely, Catholicism or Eastern Orthodoxy. In other words, they see an abandoning of what they regard as classical Protestantism. Other critics see in the dim, candlelit worship spaces something sinister and evil, a kind of dark or "new age" spirituality. They are sure that the emerging church is actually the undoing of the church, the proverbial last nail in the Western church's coffin.

We need to notice what is happening here. We are spending a great deal of energy these days worrying about the forms and media of worship. We are wrestling with whether one type of music is more appropriate than another for worship. We are debating the merits of liturgical dance. We aren't sure what to do if our church substitutes candlelight for electricity. We are questioning whether Protestants can make use of iconography without giving way to idolatry. And on and on it goes.

In the midst of all our anxiety, we need to stand back, relax, and do four things. First, we need to recall that we Christians have been worshipping our God for a very, very long time. Across the centuries and throughout the world, we have employed an amazing diversity of forms and media in our worship.[18] We have employed every musical instrument imaginable, from organs and pianos, to harps, bagpipes, drums, and a variety of horns and stringed instruments. We have used an astonishing array of music styles, ranging from chant to drumming, classical music, hymns, Southern gospel, black gospel, and hip-hop. We have used an astonishing variety of sacred art, including sculpture, wood panel paintings, frescoes, and kitsch.[19] We have worshipped our God in bright, sunlit sanctuaries and in mysterious, dark spaces. We have celebrated and praised our God in everything from caves to cathedrals.[20] We have worshipped our God at midnight and in the wee hours of the morning. We have used the lectionary, and we have preached extemporaneously. We have worn every conceivable kind of clothing, and we have stripped naked for baptism.

Second, in the light of the history of Christian worship, we need to make a very simple decision. We need to decide whether we are going to operate with a miserly or a generous pneumatology. Like prayer, *all true worship originates with the Holy Spirit.* Thus we must decide whether we are going to confine the work of the Holy Spirit to favored liturgical forms and media or whether we are going to confess together that the Holy Spirit is free to work or not to work, to speak or not to speak, to be present or not to be present regardless of the forms or media that we choose to employ.[21] We must decide whether we are going to confine the Spirit to hymns, or whether we will be open to the presence and work of the Spirit through gospel songs, praise choruses, or Byzantine chant. We must decide whether we really want to claim that the Holy Spirit is afraid of the dark, or whether we will be open to the moving of the Holy Spirit in dimly lit worship spaces.

Assuming that we are ready to confess that, across the centuries and in the present day, the Holy Spirit works in and through a wide variety of liturgical forms and media to enable the true worship of God, the third thing we need to do is to recall that worship is ultimately about God. Worship is *not about us.* It is not about getting our way. It is about the joyous celebration of God's ways with us. Indeed, whatever else we may want to say about worship, the object and focus of Christian worship is none other than the Holy Trinity. The primary

audience for our worship is Father, Son, and Holy Spirit. Along with
the whole of creation, the church exists for the celebration and glo-
rification of the Holy Trinity. We exist to celebrate and give thanks
both for the divine attributes and for the creating and saving activities
of God. We exist to celebrate and give joyous thanks for the love and
mercy and grace of the Holy Trinity and to sing praises for all God has
done in creation and for our salvation. Everything else is secondary in
importance. In fact, everything that distracts from this work, including arguments over what forms and media are acceptable for worship,
ought to be regarded with suspicion.

The fourth and final thing that we need to do is to think theologically about what it really means for worship to be Trinitarian.
We need to remind ourselves that worship is not Trinitarian simply
because we address God as Father, Son, and Holy Spirit or as Trinity.
Rather, Christian worship is Trinitarian precisely because in worship
the Holy Spirit attunes our minds and hearts to the presence of our
resurrected Lord and, incorporating us into his body, makes us one
with each other even as the Spirit and the Son are one with God the
Father (John 17). Christian worship is Trinitarian because, in worship,
the Spirit enables us to cry "Abba, Father" (Rom 8:15). In other words,
Christian worship is Trinitarian insofar as through singing hymns
and confessing our sins, through hearing the Scriptures read, and
through preaching and receiving the sacraments, we are caught up in
the Trinitarian life of God.

Given what we have just said, perhaps the question we most
need to ask ourselves today is not whether this or that instrument
is acceptable or whether the sanctuary should be brightly or dimly
lit, but how the Holy Trinity is present in and to our worship, indeed,
enabling our worship. We need to ask ourselves where and how in our
worship we are meeting the living God face to face. We need to decide
whether we are merely addressing God, or whether the Triune God is
also *addressing us*.

If the God of all creation and of our salvation is present in and
to our worship, then we have more important things to worry about
than whether the music is to our liking. If the Holy Trinity is present in and to our worship, then there is a sense in which we should
never feel entirely at home in worship, as there is something mysterious and more than a little unsettling about being in the presence of
one who is wholly unlike us and on whom we depend entirely for our

next breath. As H. Richard Niebuhr once put it, we need to remember that "we are in the grip of power that neither asks our consent before it brings us into existence nor asks our agreement to continue us in being beyond our physical death."[22]

If the Holy Trinity is present in and to our worship, then what we need to grapple with most is not what shoes are appropriate for worship, but what *dispositions* are most appropriate.[23] We need to spend more time and energy thinking about how we ought to prepare ourselves to encounter in and through worship the God who is over all creation, who is the very source of all that is and all that will be, and whose gracious generosity we are absolutely dependent on both for our ongoing existence and for our salvation. In other words, we need to spend more time and energy helping each other to worship the Holy Trinity in humility, repentance, thanksgiving, and joy.

Notice what is happening here. By reflecting theologically on the mission of worship, we have in the space of a few short pages shifted our attention from debates about what liturgical forms and media are acceptable or appropriate for Christian worship to a concern for the kind of dispositions that are most appropriate for Christian worship. Now, my suggestion is that, if we Christians would keep our focus on the concern for cultivating proper dispositions for worship, then a great deal of the tension and anxiety in and around the topic of worship would dissipate. In time, we would learn to be open to a wide variety of liturgical forms and media. Most importantly, by cultivating a disposition for worship characterized by humility, repentance, thanksgiving, and joy, we would learn to open ourselves to the transforming presence of the Holy Trinity wherever we find Christians singing praises to their God, praying the "Our Father," reading the Scriptures, proclaiming the gospel, confessing their sins, receiving the sacraments, and the like. In short, we would learn to be ever mindful that, because worship is ultimately a part of God's mission in the world, the church's role is not to control or to manage worship so much as it is *to receive it* and to be caught up in it whenever and however it breaks out among us.

Before we move to on to the second aspect of the church's mission, namely, bearing witness to Jesus Christ, we need to make one final point concerning the vast array of liturgical resources that the Spirit has given to the church across the centuries and throughout the world.[24] These resources include liturgies, sacraments, sacred images,

Holy Scripture, creeds and doctrine, the lives of the saints, and an entire range of practices related directly to the liturgy, including the practices of confession, repentance, testimony, absolution, fasting, prayer, foot-washing, preaching, praying, singing hymns, and so on. While the Holy Spirit is free to use any aspect of creation to help enable worship, I think a good case can be made that, instead of turning to popular culture for help, the church should pursue the renewal of worship initially by retrieving and redeploying her own resources. To be sure, the so-called emerging church movement is moving in this direction, but there is much more to be done on this front.[25]

There are at least two reasons to prefer the vast resources that the church has received from the Holy Spirit across the centuries and around the world over resources gathered in from popular culture. First, the church's resources are explicitly Christian in their content. They witness directly to the Holy Trinity and to the life, death, and resurrection of Jesus Christ. This is clearly the case, for example, in the sacraments of baptism and the Eucharist, in the Holy Scriptures, in the Creed, and in the canon of sacred images and hymns. By contrast, images, videos, and music that derive from popular culture tend to bear witness in less direct ways, and they often have to be stretched considerably to do so. This means that, apart from careful explanation and interpretation, the connection to Christianity is often lost on people in the pews. Moreover, materials, persons, and practices gathered in from popular culture initially divert attention away from the glory and grace of the Holy Trinity and from the life, death, and resurrection of Jesus Christ. Even when we work hard to make the connection clear, many people are so busy laughing at or otherwise enjoying a familiar video clip that they often miss the theological point that we are trying to make. To use more technical language, materials, persons, and practices derived from popular culture often fail to make the transition from uninterpreted signs to symbols and sacraments that point beyond themselves to the mystery and magnanimity of the Holy Trinity.[26]

The second reason to prefer the church's own resources over resources gathered in from pop culture is even more important that the first. The liturgical resources available in the life of the church are *proven* means of grace. Indeed, this is precisely why certain materials, persons, and practices have acquired canonical status across the centuries. The Holy Spirit has been persistently present and at work in and through these things, enabling persons to know, love, and worship the Holy Trinity and to be transformed in the process. To see this clearly, we need the kind of dramatic reversal of direction in our thinking that Jürgen Moltmann calls for when he writes, "It is not the church that administers the Spirit as the Spirit of preaching, the Spirit of sacraments, the Spirit of the ministry or the Spirit of tradition. The Spirit 'administers' the church with the events of word and faith, sacrament and grace, offices and traditions."[27] With this final point in place, we are ready to turn to the second part of the church's twofold mission.

Bearing Witness to Jesus Christ

If the church's mission begins with worshipping the Holy Trinity in humility, thanksgiving, and praise, then it continues in the church's witness to Jesus Christ in word and deed throughout the world. When we recall the church is by nature a charismatic community brought into existence and nurtured continuously by the Holy Spirit, we readily see that no activity is more appropriate to the church than bearing witness to Jesus Christ. To the extent that the Holy Spirit is present and at work in the church, bearing witness to Jesus Christ should come naturally, as bearing witness to Jesus Christ is what the Holy Spirit does. For example, in the New Testament, we see the Holy Spirit present and at work bearing witness to Jesus throughout Jesus' life and ministry.[28] The Spirit bears witness to Jesus at Jesus' baptism, transfiguration, and resurrection, and Jesus' entire ministry is undertaken in the presence and power in the Spirit. Furthermore, as we noted in the first chapter, Peter instinctively interprets the Spirit's descent at Pentecost as the ultimate witness to and confirmation of Jesus' resurrection.

Born of and animated by the Spirit, the church's witness to Jesus Christ originates in her worship. In her divine services, the church bears witness to Jesus in an entire host of ways, including proclamation; the celebration of the sacraments; hymnody; and in sacred images depicting the life, death, and resurrection of Jesus. Sometimes the very structure of the church bears witness to Jesus, as when churches take the shape of the cross.

Initially, we may be tempted to regard the Church's witness to Jesus Christ in worship as primarily a witness in word. After all, much of Christian worship involves the use of words. However, to the extent that church members watch over one another in love, the church's witness to Christ in deed also originates in the church's worship. Suffice it to say that watching over one another in love requires more than merely being polite on Sunday. When we Christians gather for worship, we witness to Christ in deed by demonstrating deep concern for one another's well-being in at least three crucial ways. First, we pray for one another during worship, especially when individual members are suffering or in need. Second, we give offerings during worship, in part to care for the poor among and around us. Third, we look after one another's spiritual welfare in worship by confessing our sins and granting forgiveness to one another.

If witnessing to the life, death, and resurrection of Jesus in word and deed is inherent in the church's worship, then it is also a *criterion* for right worship. If worship is to be done in, through, and by the Holy Spirit, then whatever else worship may be about, it must always be about bearing witness to Jesus Christ in word and deed. If it is in the Spirit's nature to bear witness to Jesus Christ, then it is difficult to see how worship can be of the Spirit yet lack a clear witness to Jesus Christ.

Beyond her divine services, the church extends her witness to Jesus Christ in word and deed in a variety of ways, including evangelistic and missionary activities, catechesis and spiritual formation, works of mercy and love, hospitality to strangers, care for widows and orphans, support for the diseased and dying, care for the creation, and advocacy for social justice throughout the world. Indeed, when we stand back and consider all the church does to bear witness to Jesus Christ in word and deed throughout the world, it is truly staggering. At her Spirit-filled best, the church really is salt and light in a tasteless and dark world.

Unfortunately, like the church's worship, the twofold form of the church's witness to Jesus Christ has at times been a source of deep division within the church. This division is especially problematic within Protestantism, where there is a long-standing disagreement over whether the church's witness ought primarily to be a witness in word or a witness in deed. Thus many evangelical Protestants have often given primacy to the church's witness to Jesus Christ in word, most notably in preaching, evangelism, and missionary work, whereas liberal Protestants have often given primacy to the church's worship in deed, most notably in the so-called social gospel movement, in the various forms of liberation theology in the 1960s and '70s, and in the emphasis on social justice that is so prevalent today.

When we look closely at most Protestant churches, we begin to suspect that the long-standing division over which form of witness should have primacy is at times more stereotype than reality. After all, many so-called evangelical churches are socially activistic, and many so-called liberal Protestant churches are evangelistic and supportive of missionary work.[29] Nevertheless, the stereotype is stubbornly persistent, and it is a constant threat to church unity and cooperation for the sake of the gospel of Jesus Christ. Thus evangelicals often assume that churches that talk a lot about social justice are not committed to the work of evangelism, whereas liberal or progressive Protestants who are deeply committed to social justice often assume that evangelicals are indifferent toward the needs of the world.[30]

At a deeper level, the *content* of the church's witness reveals a real dispute, if not outright division, within the church. The issue here is christological. In modern and postmodern Christianity, there is a deep and ongoing dispute over the person and work of Jesus Christ.[31] There is strong disagreement over the identity and significance of the One to whom the church bears witness in word and deed. Thus some insist that the church's witness is to the Christ of the ecumenical creeds and councils, while others are calling upon the church to bear witness to the historically reconstructed Jesus of Nazareth beloved by modern biblical scholars.[32] When it comes to the doctrine of the atonement, some are insisting that Christ's suffering and death were necessary for our salvation, while others are advocating for a nonviolent theory of the atonement.[33]

Clearly, we cannot resolve here the deep internal disputes over the person and work of Jesus Christ. These disputes are hardly new, persisting as they have both within and without the church from the beginning.[34] It would be foolish to think we could say anything in our theological reflections on church renewal that would put an end to these long-standing disagreements.

What we can do, however, is to recall a very important theological principle known simply as *lex orandi, lex credendi*. This well-known principle is often translated "the rule of worship [is] the rule of belief."

For our purposes, we might say *the rule of worship is the rule of witness*. In other words, how we think about and approach Jesus Christ in worship will determine what we say about Jesus Christ in our witness. If we worship Jesus Christ as fully God by addressing our hymns and prayers to him, then we will be more likely to bear witness in word and deed to One who is fully God. We will proclaim in word that the fullness of Jesus' divinity means he has *the power to save* and to heal us, and we will bear witness to the fullness of Jesus' divinity in deed by *obeying* his commands (we will receive his commandments and instructions as commandments and instructions from God). Similarly, if we celebrate and give joyous thanks that the second person of the Trinity became incarnate for us and for our salvation, then we will be more likely to bear witness in word and deed to the fullness of Jesus' humanity by announcing and embodying the faith, hope, and love that only the incarnation makes possible. By contrast, if we do not worship Jesus Christ as fully divine and fully human, then we will be unlikely to bear witness in word and deed to the fullness of Jesus' divinity or the fullness of his humanity. We will either bear witness to one who has no real power to make a difference in the world, or we will bear witness to one who has supreme power but who cannot relate to the human situation and whose power therefore is not constrained by mercy and love. We will bear witness to a mere moral teacher whose advice can be taken on merit, or we will bear witness to an all-powerful deity who is more likely to deploy his power for our destruction than to give it up for us and for our salvation.[35]

If we take seriously the theological principle, *lex orandi, lex credendi*, then it ought to give us pause in our quest for renewal. We ought to slow down and think theologically about the changes we are making in our worship. In this case, we are not talking about the changes to the media or instruments used in worship. As we have already seen, the Holy Spirit has enabled Christian worship through a wide range of media, instruments, music, and sacred art across the centuries, and it is safe to say that the Spirit continues to do so today. Rather, we need to think theologically about what we are saying about Jesus Christ in our preaching and in our singing, in iconography and in the sacraments, and so on. Instead of ignoring Christology as a matter of pedantic, academic debates that have little bearing on how we live, we need to reflect carefully on the reasons that the church canonized doctrines about Jesus at Nicaea and Chalcedon. We need to think carefully about why the church insisted that Jesus was fully divine from eternity, as well as fully human in every way except without sin. Far from being unrelated to how we live, these teachings about Jesus convey that he has not only the power to save but that he also understands *our need* for salvation.

In many quarters today, a growing concern over the freefall in church membership and worship attendance is prompting knee-jerk reactions. Out of a sense of urgency, we rush to overhaul the church's worship from top to bottom. In the process, we update the technology and media, but we also play fast and loose with the content of the church's worship. For example, it is not uncommon for clergy to take an entirely casual approach to the Eucharist, emphasizing that there is nothing special about the elements and failing altogether to invoke the Holy Spirit to come and to make the ordinary into something truly extraordinary, namely, a means of healing and holiness. As a result, any lively sense of the real presence of Christ in the Eucharist is rapidly diminishing in many quarters. Similarly, it is all too common to pray and pronounce benedictions in the name of God the creator, redeemer, and sustainer rather than in the name of God the Father, Son, and Holy Spirit with little regard for the fact that the God adumbrated by creator, redeemer, and sustainer has more in common with the God of Sabellianism or modalism than with the Holy Trinity of ecumenical Christianity.

In the ongoing quest for renewal, we need to be clear and consistent in the application of *lex orandi, lex credendi.* We need to worship Jesus as one who is fully divine, and we need to obey his commands to preach the gospel and to care for the poor. We need to celebrate and to give thanks that Jesus, though fully divine, became incarnate and dwelled among us as one who is fully human, giving up all that was rightly his so that we might know that God is love—that when we are in need, we really do have an advocate with God (1 John 4).

To worship Jesus as fully God and fully human means that we cannot rest content with a witness in word through preaching and evangelism that fail to give equal energy to a witness in deed through works of love and social justice. Nor can we content ourselves with a witness in deed that is divorced from a witness of word. If it is none other than God who commands us both to make disciples and to care for the least of these, then we have no choice but to give ourselves to the work of witness in word *and* deed and thereby to resist the stereotypes that so readily attend these activities. In other words, evangelical Protestants who worship Jesus as divine must do evangelism *and* work for social justice. Likewise, liberal or progressive Protestants who worship Jesus as divine must fight for the oppressed *and* spread the good news that Jesus Christ is truly Lord. Similarly, if the one who commands us is also the one who became incarnate for us and for our salvation, then we must bear witness to him in word and deed in a spirit of humility, grace, and love, doing all that we can not only to witness *to* those who do not yet believe but also to speak *with* them and *for* them. In other words, the humanity of Christ means that our witness in word and deed must be loving and kind rather than judgmental and harsh.

Finally, we should conclude our reflections on the work of witness by noting two important similarities with the work of worship. First, like the work of worship, *the work of witness originates with the Holy Spirit.* In and of ourselves, we are simply not capable of bearing witness to Jesus Christ (1 Cor 12:3). Thus whether we are preparing to witness to Jesus Christ in word or in deed, we should begin by invoking the Holy Spirit to enable us to do so truthfully and effectively. Second, like the work of worship, the Spirit has enabled the church to carry out the work of witness in word and deed across the centuries and throughout the world through an astonishing array of media. Once again, what is needed is a generous rather than a miserly pneumatology. Instead of confining the work of witness to favored and familiar methods and procedures (e.g., revivals, camp meetings, tracts, sit-ins, marches, and the like), we should invite the Holy Spirit to open our eyes and our imaginations to both old and new ways of bearing witness to Jesus Christ in word and deed, including contemplative ways of bearing witness that have long flourished in the Christian mystical tradition and the more recent possibilities for bearing witness through the Internet and other social networking media.[36]

The Mission of the Church and the Quest for Renewal

In this chapter, we have been working to construct a theological vision of the church's mission that can help to guide and to stimulate our thinking about renewal. We have suggested that the church exists primarily, if not exclusively, to worship the Holy Trinity and to bear witness to the life, death, and resurrection of Jesus Christ in word and deed. Going forward, we should make our decisions concerning the renewal of the church with this vision in mind. Indeed, we can do worse than, while tarrying together in prayer, to ask the Holy Spirit to help us to discern whether a particular decision or action will enable the church more *faithfully* to worship the Holy Trinity and more *effectively* to bear witness to Jesus Christ in word and deed in our local communities and throughout the world. For example, when we consider things like hiring staff, relocating, adding new technology, updating our worship, or taking on a social cause, we need to identify how these things will help the church more faithfully to worship the Holy Trinity and more effectively to bear witness to Jesus.

From the standpoint of the mission of the church, the problem with renewal is not that we lack for good ideas or suggestions. On the contrary, our problem is that we have a superabundance of suggestions for how we ought to go about renewing the church in its mission. In fact, for every concrete suggestion that someone makes, we can easily find another person suggesting that the church should do the opposite. Consider the examples that we have just mentioned. For every person who suggests that hiring highly trained staff is a key to renewing the church in its mission, another person will suggest that the path to renewal lies not in hiring staff but in training the laity. Similarly, for every renewal advocate who endorses relocation to high-visibility properties in the suburbs as a path to renewal, we can readily find someone insisting that the church should remain in undesirable, crime-ridden neighborhoods in the inner city. Likewise, for every prophetic leader or movement that urges the church to acquire and to use the latest technology, there is a prophetic leader or movement urging the church to forgo technology in favor of more natural, earth-hewn symbols and media. Finally, for every renewal advocate who endorses the contemporizing of the church's worship, someone else will insist that the church should be working to recover ancient liturgical practices.

Amid so many contrasting proposals for what the church should do in order more faithfully and more effectively to carry out its mission in the world, the temptation is to think that there must be one and only one "right" answer. However, this may not be the case. If we can bring ourselves to operate from the standpoint of a generous rather than a miserly pneumatology, then we will have recourse to a very different way of thinking. Instead of thinking that we must identify and implement the *one* approach to renewal that will enable the church more faithfully and effectively to carry out its mission, we can begin to think of the contrasting and competing proposals for renewal as an embarrassment of riches that reflects the creativity and generosity of the Holy Spirit. We can open ourselves to the possibility that the Holy Spirit is free to enable the church faithfully and effectively to carry out its twofold mission through a wide variety of approaches to and locations for ministry, through high and low technology, and through ancient and contemporary forms of worship.

When we begin to think in more generous ways about the Spirit's enabling of the church to carry out its mission in the world, our thinking about renewal takes the form of moral reasoning. To be sure, we often think of moral reasoning as having primarily to do with distinguishing right from wrong, good from evil, and the like. In many ways, the most difficult kind of moral reasoning happens when we undertake to choose from among a list of competing goods.[37] For example, suppose I have some free time this afternoon. There is almost an endless array of possibilities for spending that time. I could take a nap and thereby get some much-needed rest. I could spend time with my children, letting them know that I love them and enjoy being with them. Or I could spend that time volunteering at the local food bank, helping to serve the poor in my community. The same thing goes for how I spend my extra money. We could readily imagine an entire list of possibilities, all of which we might deem morally good uses of money.

All too often, we think about church renewal from a standpoint of scarcity rather than a standpoint of abundance, even superabundance. Yet if we really believe that it is not the church per se but God who has a mission, then why should we not think that God would provide the church with a superabundance of ways to participate in that mission? This does not mean that we can simply assume that God is in every proposal for renewal or that we can take a whimsical approach to the work of renewal. On the contrary, while the Holy Spirit is free to work in and through every means imaginable to bring about the renewal of the church in her mission, the Spirit is also free not to work. In other words, the freedom of the Spirit really does cut both ways.

What all of this means is that, when viewed from the standpoint of the mission of the church (which is to say, from the standpoint of the *missio Dei*), the quest for renewal is not ultimately a quest for the "right" proposal or program. Rather, the quest for renewal must be a never-ending quest (1) to discern when, where, and how the Holy Spirit is at work enabling the church to worship the Holy Trinity and to bear witness to the life, death, and resurrection of Jesus Christ; and (2) to discern the ways in which we can best join in that work. In other words, we should be wary of identifying one proposal or one program as the special provenance of the Spirit, as though the Holy Spirit can be confined to one location or one way of doing things. If anything, the history of Israel and of the church suggests that the Holy Spirit refuses at every turn to be manipulated or controlled.

It is precisely at this stage, however, that a word of warning is in order. In saying that the Holy Spirit refuses to be manipulated or controlled, we are not siding with prophetic leaders and movements against ecclesial structures. Similarly, in saying that the Holy Spirit is constantly on the move, we are not suggesting that the Spirit typically abandons the old in favor of the new, the established in favor of the emerging. On the contrary, the freedom of the Spirit includes the freedom to be present and at work through prophetic leaders and movements *and* through time-tested ecclesial structures.

Finally, few things are more damaging to the church's ability faithfully and effectively to participate in the *missio Dei* than our tendency to drive a wedge between the prophetic and the structural in the church's worship and witness. When we associate the presence and work of the Holy Spirit wholly with prophetic leaders and movements or wholly with the church's established structures, we attempt to seize control of God's mission and to make it our own. Like little children who, after receiving a gift from a parent, clutch the gift with all their might for fear that the very parent who gave it to them and who is ever ready to give them even more is now conspiring to take it away, we cling either to prophetic leaders and movements or to the church's established structures as though God is not fully capable of giving us both.

By contrast, when we approach the mission of the church from the standpoint of a generous pneumatology, we are free to relinquish control and to open ourselves to all that God is doing through prophetic leaders and movements *and* through the church's established structures. We are free to hold with open hands all that God has given to the church for the carrying out of God's mission to the world. Most importantly, amid the superabundance of gifts that God gives to the church, we are free to celebrate and to enjoy the one gift that really matters, namely, the transforming presence of the Holy Trinity in the midst of it all.

Chapter 3

The Sacramental Life of the Church

We have been thinking theologically about church renewal by reflecting on the nature and mission of the church. In chapter 1, we developed an account of the nature of the church that was grounded in the origins of the church at Pentecost and therefore in pneumatology and eschatology. In chapter 2, we developed an account of the mission of the church, according to which the Holy Spirit enables and empowers the church to worship the Holy Trinity and to bear witness to Jesus Christ in word and deed throughout the world.

In this chapter, we once again begin with a fundamental issue in ecclesiology, namely, the church's role in salvation. We will maintain that, across the centuries, leading Christian theologians, including Martin Luther and John Calvin, have taught that the church plays an *instrumental* role in salvation. We will then suggest that many evangelical and liberal Protestants today have embraced alternative views of the church either in which the church is *incidental* to salvation or in which salvation is barely mentioned at all.[1] After we identify significant theological shortcomings in these alternative views of the church, we will attempt to recover a way of understanding the church in which the church really is instrumental to salvation.

Finally, by way of introduction, we should say a brief word about the importance of thinking carefully about the desired *effects* of church renewal. Most of us think about and advocate for church renewal because we are concerned about numeric decline in the worship attendance and church membership of our local congregations and denominations. This is perfectly understandable. Numeric decline is a real and growing concern. It is not primarily a matter of poor marketing. On the contrary, numeric decline suggests that we are not doing a good job with evangelism, catechesis, and discipleship. So we are in no way suggesting that we should simply ignore numeric decline.[2]

The problem here has to do with nearsightedness. We see problems directly in front of us, but we rarely look further down the road. We do not take the time to think about what we really desire for the church over the long haul. We succumb to the tyranny of the urgent, doing whatever it takes to stave off further decline and, if possible, to increase worship attendance and church membership. In most cases, the formula for growth is simple enough. We freshen up our worship, we emphasize hospitality to the unchurched, and we work hard to create a warm and friendly environment.

Let us be clear. Clergy and laity *should* be worried about worship attendance and church membership. However, we need to address an even deeper issue. We need to put as much time and energy into thinking about *why* people should come to church as we do into thinking about *how* to get them to come. In other words, we need to think carefully about what the church actually has to offer people who come to worship or who become members. If we are not clear about why people will be better off for the trouble of getting out of bed on Sunday morning, then we may succeed in boosting attendance for a season, but we will fall short of the long-haul renewal that we so desperately need and desire.[3] This is the deep issue that we will be addressing in this chapter.

Extra Ecclesiam Nulla Salus

In addition to the nature and mission of the church, a third fundamental of ecclesiology is captured in the ancient axiom *extra ecclesiam nulla salus*. The standard translation of this axiom is "outside the church there is no salvation." In its basic form, we can trace this axiom as far back as the writings of St. Cyprian of Carthage, a bishop in the third century, and we can find either the formula itself or something close to it in the writings of numerous theologians across the centuries.

Today, many Protestant Christians associate this ancient theological axiom with Roman Catholicism and to a lesser extent with Eastern Orthodoxy, rarely stopping to inquire about its reception history in Protestantism. Over against this axiom, many Protestants assert that salvation is a personal matter having to do with faith in Jesus Christ and not with church membership or worship attendance. This sentiment is even reflected in the organization of Protestant systematic theologies. Following Christology and pneumatology, many Protestant systematic theologians turn directly to soteriology. They only take up ecclesiology after treating the doctrine of salvation extensively, leaving the impression that the church is *incidental*, rather than *instrumental*, to salvation.[4]

In stark contrast to the current tendency among many Protestant theologians, Martin Luther and John Calvin, the two leading architects of the Protestant Reformation, recognized and affirmed the theological axiom "outside the church there is no salvation." For example, Luther says,

> Therefore he who would find Christ must first find the Church. How should we know where Christ and his faith were, if we did not know where his believers are? And he who would know anything of Christ must not trust himself nor build a bridge to heaven by his own reason; but he must go to the Church, attend and ask her. Now the Church is not wood and stone, but the company of believing people; one must hold to them, and see how they believe, live and teach; they surely have Christ in their midst. *For outside of the Christian church there is no truth, no Christ, no salvation.*[5]

Similarly, John Calvin declares that for "those to whom [God] is a Father, the church must also be a mother."[6]

Now that we have established the Protestant credentials of this important theological axiom, we cannot afford to get sidetracked by the additional concerns that many people often raise when they hear this axiom. For example, many people will immediately want to know what it means to be outside or inside the church. They will want to know whether it is simply a matter of baptism, or whether there are additional requirements. If it is primarily a matter of baptism, then they will want to know whether all baptized persons will be saved regardless of how they live after their baptism. Moreover, they will want to know whether any baptism will do, or whether it is only baptism into a particular church that secures salvation. If it is only baptism into a particular church that secures salvation, then they will naturally want to know which church is the one true church into which they must be baptized in order to be saved. Some will want to know whether infant baptism counts or whether it is only adult baptism that does the job. Increasingly, people will want to know what this axiom implies about adherents to other world religions. More specifically, they will want to know whether salvation is available in Judaism, Islam, Buddhism, Hinduism, and the like. These are just some of the questions that this little axiom often provokes.[7]

For our purposes, a minimalist interpretation of the axiom will more than suffice. We do not need at this stage to take up the matter of salvation in other world religions.[8] We need only to acknowledge that, if the testimony of Christians from across the centuries and around the world is to be trusted, salvation is something that happens to us when we participate in the sacramental life of the church. According to the testimony of the saints, the Holy Spirit is present and at work through the sacramental life of the church, restoring us to the image of God; enabling us to know and love God with all of our heart, mind, soul, and strength; helping us to know how rightly to love our friends and even our enemies; reconciling us to God the Father through Jesus Christ, the eternally begotten Son; empowering us for worship and witness; and so on. Through the sacramental life of the church, the Holy Spirit forms the mind of Christ in believers; enables us to live out the theological virtues of faith, hope, and love; and transforms us into a people whose lives are characterized by things like love, joy, peace, patience, gentleness, goodness, kindness, and self-control.[9] Through the sacramental life of the church, God redeems, transforms, heals, and sanctifies us. In and through the sacramental life of the church, God fills us with the presence and power of the Holy Spirit and with all grace. In and through the sacramental life of the church, God immerses us in God's own Trinitarian life, making us perfect in ministry and in love.

For many people, the foregoing vision of the sacramental life of church will sound overly optimistic and naïve. Indeed, we can readily imagine people commenting that this vision does not sound like any church they have been to lately. Such comments, while understandable, tend to blur the line between what the church is and what she is called to be. Alternatively, they blur the line between what the church has become and what she has been and, with the help of the Holy Spirit, what she can be again.

If people do not experience the church as a place in which salvation is ever breaking in upon them, then perhaps we need to inquire about why this is the case. One possible explanation is that we were wrong to see the church as a charismatic community in which the Holy Spirit is present and at work enabling her members to pray, to worship the Holy Trinity, and to bear witness to Jesus Christ in word and deed throughout the world. In other words, we could simply say that the church has been merely a human institution from day one. Consequently, we should not expect anything more from the church than we do from any other institution.

We instinctively know that this explanation will not do. Even self-avowed atheists routinely castigate the church for not being different than any other institution. They know and we know that if the church does not bear the marks of divine activity, then she loses her very reason to be. To say that the church has never been anything more than a human institution simply will not do.

Another possible explanation is that the church began life as a charismatic community, but that because of the church's repeated sinning, the Holy Spirit withdrew from the church, leaving her to her own devices. This explanation will not do either. It simply does not cohere with what we Christians believe, teach, and confess about our God. When faced with human sin, the Holy Trinity does not run away in a huff or withdraw from us to pout. Rather, the Christian God draws near in the person of Jesus Christ, dwelling among us and eating with us. And even when we do the unthinkable, rejecting and crucifying the Son of God, God does not reject or destroy us. Rather, the Christian God is the God who keeps coming no matter what. Indeed, the Holy Trinity draws even closer. Thus the Holy Spirit comes at Pentecost not simply to dwell among us but to dwell *within* us in such a way that, as Boris Bobrinskoy once put it, "we cannot discern the frontier between his presence and our own autonomy."[10] In other words, the Holy Trinity is not prone to abandoning us when we sin. So the notion that the church is not a place where salvation is ever breaking in upon us because the Holy Spirit has withdrawn from the church doesn't even make it out of the gate.[11]

A better explanation for the loss of any robust sense that the church is a place where salvation happens is that, in many quarters, we have ceased to think about the church as instrumental to salvation. In other words, we have come to think of the church in ways that do not involve expectations of radical transformation, of holiness, and the like. Indeed, two competing visions of the church have taken the place of the vision that inheres in *extra ecclesiam nulla salus*. On the one hand, many evangelical Protestant Christians regard the church as the community of the already saved. On the other hand, many mainline liberal Protestant Christians see the church as a community of radical inclusivity.

Before we attempt to recover a vision of the church in which the church is instrumental to salvation, we need to say a little more about each of these competing views of the church. In doing so, we need to indicate why each of these views of the church is unlikely to stave off further decline or to lead to the long-haul renewal of the church in the postmodern West. However, as we turn to these competing visions of the church, a word of warning is in order. The following snapshots are *generalizations*. In both evangelical and mainline liberal Protestant circles, we can find exceptions to the accounts we are about to give. Put simply, the picture or account will not apply equally to every church. Yet, the point of a generalization is not to account for every particular case, but to identify overarching trends in a situation or the overarching sensibilities and commitments of a group of people in a way that prompts self-critical reflection. With this warning in mind, we begin with the view of the church that is now flourishing among many evangelical Protestants.

The Church as Community of the Already Saved

The notion that the church is *instrumental* or otherwise essential to salvation is one that has fallen on hard times in many quarters in the postmodern West. Among the many forces that are undermining this view of the church, the most influential may be a distinctively American form of evangelical Protestantism.[12] With roots in the

Great Awakenings and in revivalism, many twentieth- and twenty-first-century American evangelicals insist that salvation is something that takes place between individual persons and Jesus. On this rather widespread, if popular, view of salvation, people do not have to darken the doorway of a church to be saved. On the contrary, salvation is only a "sinner's prayer" away. Such a prayer can happen anywhere and anytime. It can happen in a grocery store parking lot or a movie theater, a shopping mall or an amusement park. All people need to do in order to be saved is to repent of their sins and to ask Jesus into their hearts.[13]

On this account of salvation, "being saved" or converted is equated more or less with justification or being justified. Regeneration and sanctification are often nowhere in sight. In other words, we have here a severely truncated view of salvation.

The implications of this truncated view of salvation for the vision of the church that inheres in the ancient maxim *extra ecclesiam nulla salus* are not difficult to see. At best, the church is *incidental*, not instrumental to salvation. Joining a church or being baptized are things that people do after conversion. The church is not generally thought of as a vital part of a rigorous conversion process. Rather, conversion or being saved is, like virtually everything else in the postmodern West, available on demand. It is not intimately connected to the ongoing sacramental life of the church. Rather, getting saved is the sort of thing that we can do quickly and without a great deal of effort. Far from a pearl of great price that is to be longed for and sought after, salvation is like the gumballs so readily available in supermarkets and dentists' offices. With a coin and a quick turn of the wrist, we can easily obtain the prize. Unfortunately, like the gumballs, it may turn out to be the sort of prize whose taste does not last very long.

We would be hard-pressed to overestimate how influential this view of salvation has been. We would also be hard-pressed to overestimate how theologically problematic it is. Indeed, what is really at stake in the separation of conversion and salvation from the sacramental life of the church is a theological reductionism that is spiritually disastrous. The reductionism I have in mind cuts right across the classical theological curriculum, including the doctrine of God, as well as the doctrines of human nature, sin, and salvation. Indeed, when conversion and salvation are not intimately related to the sacramental life of the church, one can expect to find a truncating of no fewer than five of the loci of systematic theology. To be sure, the theological implications are often tacit and unstated, but they are no less real and no less dangerous for it.[14]

First and foremost, when salvation is not intimately related to the sacramental life of the church, there is a truncating of the Christian doctrine of sin. This is deeply ironic, as approaches to conversion divorced from the sacramental life of the church typically begin with the doctrine of original sin and total depravity, registering the need for forgiveness, for relief of one's debt to God, for pardon from punishment, and the like. The reductionism occurs not because sin is left out, but because the true nature and consequences of sin are not carefully considered. More specifically, the nature and consequences of sin are often conceived in exclusively legal or juridical terms. Sin has to do with the transgressing of divine laws and not with the disordering of human desire and human love. What is missing here is what Ellen Charry, following Augustine, refers to as the "struggle to know, love, and enjoy God"—a struggle that is "basic to human life." Indeed, the struggle to know and love God is "the one from which all other struggles arise and into which they dissolve."[15]

As Charry notes, the deep issue here has to do with "the ambiguity of love and the instability of desire." The human struggle with sin is, at its root, a struggle with the disordering of the self that is a direct result of disordered desire and disordered love. Indeed, disordered desire and disordered love are the sources of "our misery and suffering in this life."[16] In other words, we desire and we love all sorts of things *as if they were God*. Consequently, we fail to desire and to love the one thing that will truly bring happiness, namely, the knowledge, love, and enjoyment of God.

Unfortunately, we have not reached the end of the matter. An even deeper problem is our inability to do anything about the situation in which we find ourselves. We continually desire and love all sorts of things as though they were God, regardless of how many times the things that we love and desire turn out to be disappointments. We continually seek enjoyment and true happiness in all the wrong places. Despite the reassurances of modern psychology, we cannot save ourselves.[17]

When we separate conversion and salvation from the life of the church, these dimensions of the "human situation" are often nowhere in sight. The point of conversion is to secure forgiveness and pardon for our sins, but sin here is clearly a matter of having done the wrong thing. Unfortunately, loving and desiring the wrong thing is an even more intractable and debilitating problem than doing the wrong thing.[18]

At this stage, we are already in the territory of the second theological reductionism accompanying understandings of conversion and salvation that are not intimately related to the sacramental life of the church. Reductionistic views of sin mask reductionistic views of human nature. The psychology at work is unbearably thin, foregrounding human intellect and will quite apart from passion and desire, not to mention the deep springs from which human desires flow. The basic scheme works like this. Human persons somehow know God's law (the intellectual component), but they consistently choose to disobey God's law (the volitional component). What is missing is any sustained reflection on *why* human beings willfully disobey the laws of God. More specifically, what is missing from this account of human psychology is an appreciation of the extent to which human persons are creatures of passion and desire.[19] Before we will, we desire. Before we act, we love. Unfortunately, many of our desires and loves are misplaced. Either we desire the wrong thing or we desire things in inappropriate ways or to an inappropriate degree. This includes our desires for food, sex, political power, and celebrity status. Even more important are the deep springs from which misplaced human desires or disordered human loves flow. If we break God's laws, then we do not do so because of a failure of will, as though being human were primarily a matter of grit and determination. Our problem is much deeper than that.

A third kind of theological reductionism follows naturally from reductionistic views of human nature and sin, namely, reductionistic views of atonement and of salvation. On this account, what human persons need is pardon for transgression and the appeasement of the demands of God's righteousness. The good news is that Jesus Christ has taken our place in meeting the demands of righteousness. Christ literally stands in for us as a substitute, suffering the punishment that is our due.[20] In doing so, he secures pardon for our sins. Thus many evangelical Protestants often construe salvation as pardon, as relief from debt, and so on.[21] Overcoming the real problem that haunts humanity—the problem of disordered love and disordered desire—is nowhere in sight.

A fourth area of theological reductionism has to do with our role in salvation. When we separate conversion from the sacramental life of the church, we must do two things to lay claim to salvation (construed as pardon for sin). Put simply, we must confess our guilt, and we must confess Jesus Christ is Lord. Upon making these two confessions, we are converted or saved. Again, coming to grips with the problem of disordered love and disordered desire is not part of the equation, except insofar as loving and desiring the wrong things resulted in actions worthy of divine punishment. Apart from the sacramental life of the church, our role in conversion and in salvation is reduced from a deep struggling with the problem of disordered desire to a simple confession of guilt and a request for pardon. Thus many evangelical Protestants are often quick to say that being converted or getting saved is something simple or even easy to do.[22]

The fifth and final area of reductionism has to do with the almost complete absence of the person and work of the Holy Spirit. On many evangelical Protestant accounts, the Holy Spirit's role in conversion and salvation is reduced to an epistemic one. The Spirit confirms that the doctrines or original sin, total depravity, substitutionary atonement, and salvation as pardon are true. The Holy Spirit's working through the means of grace to help us to see that only God will ultimately satisfy our deepest desires is often obscured from sight.

We can now begin to see how the vision of the church as incidental to salvation can and has contributed to the decline of the church in the postmodern West. When evangelical Protestants present salvation as something easy to obtain rather than as something that is to be worked out in fear and trembling with the help of the Holy Spirit in the company of believers, the church is devalued from the beginning. Even when evangelical Protestants insist on the importance of postconversion worship attendance and church membership, it is far from clear that such things are *ultimately* important or necessary. What is ultimately important is already, as they say, in the bag. Salvation is a done deal. At best, the church is a place to go following one's conversion and preceding one's death and entrance into eternity. In other words, the church is a sort of waiting room for heaven, the community of the already saved.

Given this view of the church, we should not be surprised that many evangelical congregations focus their marketing efforts on the wide range of social activities that they have to offer. If believers are not gathering together primarily to work out their salvation with fear and trembling before the Lord (because salvation is a fait accompli), then churches must come up with a wide range of activities that will help to hold their members' attention for another year. Rather than promoting the vital relationship between the church and salvation, many evangelical congregations advertise a trinity of food, fellowship, and fun. The message could not be clearer. The church is like a local brew pub. It is a good place to get something to eat and make a few new friends while we wait to be called home to glory.

On the slightly more high-minded side of the scale, many evangelical churches market their political and social activism. Thus the church is like any other not-for-profit organization in the community. It is a good place to come together for civic involvement or perhaps even for political caucusing.[23]

Not a few evangelical churches advertise themselves as societies for the promotion of self-esteem. People should come to church in order to improve their self-image or self-worth. The best news is that no real change is necessary. People simply need to change the way they think about themselves; they need to see that God loves them just the way they are.[24]

The problem with the foregoing ways of attracting people to the church is that they do not call attention to the vital relationship between the sacramental life of the church and salvation. They say next to nothing about the long-haul sanctifying effects of our participation in the sacramental life of the church. Rather, they emphasize the church's ability to give us temporary relief from loneliness or boredom, to provide quality entertainment, or to give us an additional avenue to pursue our political and social concerns. In and of themselves, none of these things are inherently bad. On the contrary, it is good to make new friends, to enjoy quality music, and to be socially and politically engaged. The problem is that people can pursue and obtain all of these goods without ever having to get out of bed on Sunday morning. In the postmodern West, there is no shortage of places to meet new friends, to be entertained, and to get involved in political and social causes.

The question that now lingers in the air is whether the church has anything unique to offer. As baby boomers contemplate giving the church a second chance, their children and grandchildren are beginning to inquire about the church for the first time. Sadly, many of them are finding little in the way of answers for their deepest questions and direction for their unfulfilled desires. There are plenty of doughnuts to be eaten, but these are not sufficient to nourish the growing spiritual and theological appetites of people living in the postmodern West.

Unfortunately, the vision of the church as the community of the already saved is not the only vision of the church in the postmodern West that fails to make the connection between the sacramental life of the church and the journey of salvation. A competing vision of the church is currently on offer in many liberal Protestant churches and denominations. We need to take a moment to explore this view more fully. More specifically, we need to see whether this view of the church is more likely than the view of the church as the community of the already saved to lead to the long-haul renewal of the church.

The Church as Community of Radical Inclusivity

If the vision of the church as a community of the already saved often informs the ways in which evangelical Protestant congregations market themselves, then the vision of the church as a community of radical inclusivity regularly informs liberal Protestant advertising campaigns. For example, a few years ago The United Methodist Church invested enormous amounts of time and money in a marketing campaign designed to reassure people that The United Methodist Church is above all a church that practices openness. Through television commercials, the Internet, tee-shirts, and bumper stickers, we told anyone and everyone who would listen that The United Methodist Church had "open hearts, open minds, open doors." If visitors would only bother to come, they would soon discover that United Methodists are very nice people who do not make judgments about other people's lives. On the contrary, we are committed to accepting people just as they are.

We can easily detect the view of the church behind this marketing campaign. The church is not a holy community full of saints, but a rather mundane gathering of sinners. It is not a community of mutual confession and repentance, of forgiveness and liberation, of radical conversion, or of sanctification and perfection in love for God and neighbor.[25] Rather, the church is a group of nice folks who promise not to meddle in one another's business. We are card-carrying members of what Kendra Creasy Dean recently dubbed "the cult of nice."[26]

If The United Methodist Church was attempting through its marketing campaign to stymie five decades of decline in worship attendance and church membership, then it is now clear that we bet on the wrong horse. Despite pouring enormous amounts of time and money into an advertising campaign carefully designed to say nothing substantial about God or about salvation, United Methodist worship attendance and membership have continued to trend downward.[27] We should not be surprised. People can readily find openness and tolerance at any numbers of clubs and bars or at any number of volunteer organizations, none of which require them to get out of bed early on Sunday mornings.

The reenvisioning of the church as a community of radical inclusivity, while detectable in liberal Protestant marketing campaigns, is hardly limited to them. On the contrary, we can readily detect this view of the church in the language of liberal Protestant clergy, laity, and seminary professors. For example, Letty Russell, a liberal Protestant theologian who was known for her work in ecclesiology, defined the church as "a community *where everyone is welcome.*"[28] Indeed, the vision of the church as a community of radical inclusivity is now instantiated in what we might call new marks of the church. Like the marks of the church identified in the Nicene Creed, the new marks of the church are four in number. They are, in no particular order, inclusivity, openness, tolerance, and diversity. More than popular buzzwords, these four terms have acquired a kind of confessional status among many liberal Protestants. They represent what many liberal Protestants believe most deeply with respect to both the church and the Christian life.

If we are to assess the new marks of the church, then we need first to take a moment to revisit the old marks of the church. To be sure, the old marks do not sound as culturally sensitive or politically trendy as the new ones. For example, when compared with inclusivity and diversity, apostolicity and holiness sound antiquated and judgmental. So we can easily understand why many liberal Protestant or progressive Christians who are worried about church decline and who are working for church renewal find the new marks more appealing. The old marks involve an unfamiliar language that purportedly turns people off to the church, whereas the new marks are supposed to make the church sound more attractive to people living in the twenty-first century.[29]

At the outset, the temptation to give up on the old marks is a strong one. We must admit, however, that the old marks have been around for a long time. They have had a good run for their money. If for no other reason than their longevity, we should at least give them a proper funeral. We should take a moment to inquire about what the old marks signify. We should pause long enough to recall the vision of the church from which they originally sprang. We should think carefully about what, if anything, might be lost if we allow the new marks to replace the old.

To get at the meaning of the old marks of the church, we must first take the word *church* seriously. After all, the old marks are adjectives that modify the noun *church*. We must begin here because the meaning of adjectives can change depending upon the noun they are called upon to modify. For example, the word "hot" means one thing in the phrase "a hot *stove*" and something rather different in the phrase "a hot *car*." Presumably, the same thing is true of the adjectives *one*, *holy*, *catholic*, and *apostolic*. Thus the word "holy" means one thing in the phrase "holy church" and something else in the expression "holy cow!"

In chapter 1, we dealt rather extensively with the nature of the church. Keeping in mind all that we said there, we now need to push our understanding of the church one step further. In particular, we need to flesh out what we mean when we say that, in and through the church, the Holy Spirit incorporates us into the Trinitarian life of God.

A good way to begin thinking about what it means to be incorporated into the Trinitarian life of God is to focus our thinking on a scriptural metaphor for the church, namely, the body of Christ (1 Cor 12:27). After all, to be incorporated is to be introduced into and made an integral part of a body. To be sure, as we noted in chapter 1, the Scriptures use an entire range of metaphors to describe the church. They refer to the church as a city on a hill, the called-out ones, resident aliens, branches of the true vine, a royal city, the spotless bride of Christ, and the light of the world, to name a few. Yet the body of Christ is arguably the metaphor that has been most central theologically and liturgically down through the ages. Across the centuries, theologians have insisted that the church is not just any body. The church is not simply a voluntary collection of like-minded individuals. Nor is the church simply a community of persons who share a common story and common practices. Rather, the church is the body of Christ. In creating the church, the Holy Spirit incorporates us into the Trinitarian life of God by joining us in intimate, albeit mysterious ways to the body of Jesus Christ, most notably through partaking of Holy Eucharist.

If we are to take seriously the notion that the church is the body of Christ, then we must first inquire after what kind of body Christ has.[30] The temptation, of course, is to think of Christ's body as representative of his humanity and that exclusively. In other words, Christ's physical body is the human component of the incarnation. At a certain level, this makes sense. After all, Christ's body is broken and ultimately succumbs to death. Naturally, we want to associate brokenness and death exclusively with the humanity of Christ, preserving the dignity and purity of Christ's divinity. God, we tell ourselves, is surely not capable of suffering and dying.[31] Thus our tendency is to associate the suffering and death of Christ with the human body that Christ acquires in the incarnation.

While we instinctively want to associate Christ's broken body with his human nature, the leading theologians of the early church ultimately rejected the notion that we can neatly separate the human nature from the divine nature in Christ.[32] Rather, they insisted that Christ's human and divine natures, while distinct, were united in such a way as to make them inseparable. Most importantly, they pointed out that God brought about the union of the divine and human natures in Christ in order to heal human nature from brokenness and death.

When we think about the church as body of Christ, we need to keep in mind all that the church has said concerning Christ's two natures. As the body of Christ, the church is not immune to brokenness or even to death. On the contrary, the church is a place in which brokenness is front and center. Every time the church celebrates the Eucharist, her members are reminded that Christ's body is a broken body. They are reminded of *the deadly effects of sin.* This is the offense

of the incarnation. In Christ, God joins God's self to human brokenness, even to the point of death. As the body of Christ, brokenness is a
part of the very *nature* of the church. Brokenness is also a part of the
church's *mission*. Thus the church welcomes the poor and downtrod-
den. The church opens her doors to those broken by sin, by addiction,
and by all forms of abuse. The church is home to *all* people, regardless
of the source or shape of their brokenness.

Already, we can see some implications for how we understand
the old marks of the church. For example, as the body of Christ, the
church is *catholic* insofar as she welcomes all people, no matter how
broken. Similarly, as the body of Christ, the church is *one* insofar as all
of her members share a common human nature broken by sin.

At the same time, we must be careful to recall that, in Christ,
human nature is joined inseparably to divinity. Two natures are
united in one person, one broken and dying, the other healing and
alive. Thus, as the body of Christ, the church is not merely a human
community. On the contrary, she is joined mysteriously to the divine
nature in Christ every time she celebrates the Eucharist.

Here, too, we can see implications for how we understand the old
marks of the church. In the body of Christ, broken human nature is
united to the healing power of Christ's divine nature. To be a part
of the church is to be made *holy*. In and through participation in the
means of grace, broken persons experience divine healing, beginning
a journey toward health and wholeness.[33] Thus while the church is *one*
in brokenness and death, she is also *one* in healing and the holiness of
life that results from her union with the divine nature in Christ.

We can even see implications for how we understand apostolicity,
the last of the old marks of the church. To be sure, we often associate apostolicity with apostolic succession. According to the doctrine
of apostolic succession, there is an unbroken line of persons extend-
ing from Christ all the way down to present-day elders in the church.
Among other things, this unbroken line is said to ensure doctrinal
purity. However, in light of what we have been saying concerning the
church as the body of Christ, there may be another way to think about
apostolicity.

As the body of Christ, the church is one in brokenness and in
holiness. Apostolicity testifies to the healing power of Christ's body,
insofar as those who accept responsibility for church leadership are

exemplars of Christ's holiness. Like Paul, they model their lives after Christ so that others can model their lives after them (1 Cor 11:1). In Christ, their lives are a testimony to what happens when broken human nature is united with the divine. Indeed, we have an entire theological vocabulary for dealing with this, including the language of *theosis*, sanctification, holiness, perfection, and even transfiguration.

As attributes of the church *as body of Christ*, the old marks of the church are highly instructive for the church's nature and mission. They also make clear that the church plays an instrumental role in salvation. The church is a place in which all people are welcome.[34] The church does not flinch at brokenness and death any more than the One whose body she is. As the body of Christ, the church bears visible wounds, even mortal wounds. Her members are one in brokenness and in the death that is the wages of sin, both her own sin and the sin of others (Rom 6:23). In this respect, the church is truly *catholic* or universal.

Yet the church is also a place of radical healing and holiness. The church is a place of incorporation into the Trinitarian life of God. In and through the sacramental life of the church, the Holy Spirit unites the church's members with Jesus Christ and, in him, with God the Father. In this union, the church's members embark on a journey from brokenness to holiness. Their wounds are bound up, and they become the image of Christ on earth. As with Christ's own body, reminders of the wounds remain.[35] But there is something more. There is deep healing. There is restoration to God. There is perfect love for God and neighbor. People are no longer the same. The church is *holy* and *apostolic*.

In light of the two natures of Jesus Christ, the church's nature and mission involves both *welcoming* all who are broken and *waiting patiently with* the broken for the Holy Spirit to bind up their wounds in Christ. Brokenness is fully expected. But so is healing. This is truly good news.

When we compare them with this rich theological vision of the nature and mission of the church and of the church's instrumental role in the journey of salvation, the new marks of the church are clearly deficient. On the one hand, inclusivity, diversity, tolerance, and openness capture important aspects of oneness and catholicity. Indeed, the new marks make it clear that all people are welcome in the church. However, the new marks fail to remind people of the heal-ing power of the church. Thus we can only too easily take the new marks to suggest that people should come as they are and remain as they are. The new marks simply do not capture all that the Holy Spirit makes available to us in the church through the life, death, and resur-rection of Christ. The new marks provide one vital aspect of the good news, but they do not tell the whole story.

At this stage, we should say a brief word about the origins of the new marks of the church. The new marks of the church appear to be at least partly a result of a failure on the part of the church to emphasize both the human and divine natures of the One whose body she is. Across the centuries, many Protestant churches have exhibited a tendency to stress holiness over catholicity and oneness in sanctity over oneness in brokenness. We can even see a tendency in much Protestant worship to rush from Good Friday to Easter Sun-day, which is to say, from a theology of the cross to a theology of glory. To the extent that this happens, we do not need to invent or adopt new marks of the church. Rather, we need simply to take the old marks more seriously. The church is the body of Christ, wounds and all. The old marks remind us of the wounds; they also remind us of all that is ours in Christ. The old marks make it clear that all are welcome; they also make it clear that, in Christ, the Holy Spirit makes us truly alive in God.

For some, the motivation for inventing and promoting new marks of the church has to do with a suspicion that any and all talk of salva-tion is manipulative and coercive. To stress things like conversion and transformation is to justify theologically the reduction of the other to the same. It is to privilege and to impose our beliefs about ethics and about the good upon others. It is a means of marginalization, not a means of grace.

Unfortunately, we may have here a difference of perspective that really does go all the way down. We either believe that we have been joined to Christ and that this joining makes a real difference in how we live or we don't. We either believe in the presence and power of the Holy Spirit to bring about the transformation of human lives and communities or we don't. We either believe that the church embod-ies "in its own life the mystery of salvation and the *transfiguration of humanity*" or we don't.[36] We either trust the testimony of the saints or we don't.

Finally, we need to reiterate that, like the vision of the church as a community of the already saved, the vision of the church as a community of radical inclusivity is not likely to lead to the long-haul renewal of the church. On the contrary, these two views of the church will serve only to encourage temporary or spotty church attendance. After all, people do not need to get out of bed early on Sunday to find food, fellowship, and fun, or to find people who are inclusive, open, tolerant, and diverse. They can find all of this and more in Las Vegas casinos or in Times Square. They can find it in their local pubs and at collegiate and professional sporting events amid their fellow fans. They can find it at the beach or at any number of vacation resorts. If we want people to take the church seriously, then we must recapture a vision of church that stresses what it is that the church has to offer that cannot be readily found elsewhere, namely, salvation, transformation, and deep healing.

The Church as Spiritual Hospital

A much more helpful way to think about and to promote the church is to follow the lead of St. John of Damascus, a Syrian monk and priest who lived in the late seventh and early eighth centuries. According to St. John, the church is a spiritual hospital in and through which God works to bring about our healing, which is to say our salvation (the Greek word for salvation also means healing). Moreover, says St. John, God has endowed the church with an entire range of medicines through the taking of which the Holy Spirit restores us to God, enables us to desire and to enjoy God above all other things, brings about our spiritual healing, makes us holy, and the like. Consider for example what St. John says about the healing power of sacred images. He writes,

> Suppose I have few books, or little leisure for reading, *but walk into the spiritual hospital—that is to say, a church*—with my soul choking from the prickles of thorny thoughts, and thus afflicted I see before me the brilliance of the icon. I am refreshed as if in a verdant meadow, and thus my soul is led to glorify God. I marvel at the martyr's endurance, at the crown he won, and inflamed with burning zeal I fall down to worship God through His martyr, and so receive salvation.[37]

At this juncture, we do not need to get hung up on whether icons of saints are among the forms of medicine available to us in the life of the church. Clearly, in Eastern Orthodox Christianity, sacred images of saints play a vital role in worship and therefore in the journey of salvation. The point here is simply that, when we think of the church first and foremost as a spiritual hospital, we naturally begin to regard the various materials, persons, and practices available within the church as forms of medicine by which the Holy Spirit joins us to Christ, heals us of our sins, and transforms us to newness of life. We should not be alarmed by the fact that there is some variation in the forms of medicine available in the churches.[38] The more important thing by far is that we learn once again to think about the church's many resources as medicinal in nature and function. Scripture, baptism and Eucharist, worship, hymns and prayers, preaching and teaching, the creeds and other confessional materials, the lives of the saints, theology and doctrine, and the various mechanisms of oversight—all of these things are gifts of the Holy Spirit in and through which the Spirit works to heal our minds, bodies, and souls, and to incorporate us into the Trinitarian life of God.

The attentive reader will notice that we are deploying an image of the Holy Spirit as divine physician. This is an altogether natural image. After all, we routinely speak of the Spirit comforting us, healing our divisions, binding up our wounds, convicting us of our sins, assuring us of our forgiveness in Christ, and sanctifying us in the truth. Like an earthly physician, the Spirit accomplishes all of these things through the prescription and application of medicine appropriate to our needs. Also like an earthly physician, the Spirit routinely utilizes assistants in the work of healing. Thus we can learn once again to think of clergy and mature believers in the church as attendees or midwives of the Holy Spirit. As the divine physician, the Spirit invites us to participate in the work of healing through reading the Scriptures, sharing our faith, administering the sacraments, preaching and praying, passing on the teaching of the apostles, assisting one another in confessing our sins and announcing forgiveness, anointing the sick, reaching out to the wider community through works of mercy and social justice, and helping one another more fully to know, love, and thoroughly enjoy the grace of the Holy Trinity in the midst of it all.

The next thing to note about the vision of the church as hospital and the Holy Spirit as divine physician is the implication that human persons suffer from all manner of sickness. We suffer physically, emotionally, intellectually, and spiritually. We suffer from pride, selfishness, resentment, jealousy, greed, and disordered desires and affections. Either we love the wrong things or we love things to an inappropriate degree and in inappropriate ways. We routinely love ourselves and our interests more than we love God or our neighbors. In other words, we are not attempting here to deny or to paper over the extent of our sins through the rhetoric of inclusivity. On the contrary, when we think of the church first and foremost as a hospital and the Holy Spirit as a divine physician, we are taking even more seriously the radical evil and suffering so persistent in our world. We are recognizing that people are in desperate need of intellectual, emotional, and spiritual formation. Most importantly, we are calling attention to our collective need of the healing and restorative power of the Holy Spirit in every aspect of our lives. If the Holy Spirit is present and at work in the church, then it is not for our amusement and entertainment, our political agendas and ideologies, or our fortune and fame. Rather, the Holy Spirit is present and at work in the church rescuing people and communities from the destructiveness of sin, healing people and communities of their brokenness and dysfunction, and restoring people and communities to joyous communion with the Holy Trinity, with their friends and with their enemies, indeed, with the whole of creation.

Here, then, is our situation. We are not lacking for resources in the church to help us to come clean about and then to combat any and all sins, including the social sins of racism, sexism, ethnocentrism, and classism. On the contrary, we have an abundance of resources in and through which the Holy Spirit works to enable us openly and freely to confess our sins to one another, to cleanse us of all unrighteousness, and to make us a holy people.[39] It is not that we have too little with which to work but that we have too much. The church is the recipient of an embarrassment of riches. The Holy Spirit has given us more than we could ask for or imagine for the purpose of restoring us to communion with the Holy Trinity and with one another. For example, we do not just have one book. We have an entire library of books, totaling sixty-six in all. When we add to the canonical Scriptures the inter-testamental books, the writings of church fathers and mothers, creeds and confessions, and the writings of the great theologians across the centuries, we discover we have a wealth of written materials in and through which the Holy Spirit convicts us of our sins, assures us of forgiveness, reconciles us to God and neighbor, fills our hearts with all grace, sanctifies our minds and hearts, and makes us alive unto God.

In addition to written materials, the Holy Spirit is present and at work through an entire range of sacred practices, including prayer, preaching and teaching, worship, baptism and Eucharist, fasting, testimony, anointing, foot-washing, tithing and almsgiving, love feasts, missions and evangelism, confession and absolution, singing hymns, and meditating upon sacred images. In and through these ecclesial practices, the Holy Spirit cleanses us from our sins; heals our broken hearts and lives; reorients our lives to God; restores and sanctifies our sight; and inculcates in us the virtues of faith, hope, and love. Far from mundane and outdated, the practices at the core of the church's life across the centuries are *spiritually explosive*. To take them seriously is to invite the Holy Spirit to bring about a revolution in the church and in our lives.

Similarly, the Holy Spirit is present and at work through a range of persons, including the clergy and mature believers, bishops and other persons charged with episcopal oversight, and a long and highly diverse line of saints. In and through these persons, the Spirit works to pass on the faith to each new generation, enabling them truly to worship the Holy Trinity and to bear witness to Jesus Christ in word and deed throughout the world. Rightly understood, episcopal leaders are not grossly overpaid administrators. They are vital means of grace and living channels through which the Holy Spirit is present and at work in the life of the church. Likewise, the saints are not merely persons worthy of our admiration. They are persons whom the Holy Spirit calls us to emulate in preparation for baptism and in ongoing discipleship and training in the faith.

In the postmodern West, the church is beset by two problems. First, in many quarters, we have lost confidence in the materials, persons, and practices that the Holy Spirit has given to the church for our healing and our salvation. We have lost confidence in the power of the Scriptures and the sacraments to form and to transform our lives. We have lost confidence in the power of Spirit-filled preaching and prayer to convict us of our sins and to assure us of our forgiveness. We have lost confidence in the power of the testimony of the saints to guide us into all truth. Put simply, we have lost confidence in the very resources by which the church lives and by which she is a source of the renewal of life and of holiness throughout the world.

The good news on this front is that the church's sacred materials, persons, and practices are like potent forms of medicine tucked away in a medicine cabinet. They are readily available for recovery and use. We need only to repent of our un-faith and our disbelief and to attend to what is close at hand.

The second problem is of a different sort. To recover and to redeploy all that the Holy Spirit has given to the church for our healing and our salvation can be an overwhelming task. It is not simply a matter of making sure we use everything on a list from time to time. Rather, we are going to need to exercise a great deal of discernment in the selection and deployment of the church's materials, persons, and practices. The truth is that some of these materials, persons, and practices are well-suited to beginners, while other resources are more appropriate to mature believers. Indeed, some of the church's resources are like strong medicine for which adequate preparation is crucial. So we do not need simply to begin using all the resources that the Spirit has given to the church. Rather, we need to begin using them all wisely.

In response to these two problems, two things are desperately needed. On the one hand, we desperately need to rediscover for ourselves the power and potency of the full range of resources that the Spirit has given to the church. Moreover, we need to foster a disposition of vital expectation such that whether we are preaching, praying, confessing our sins, receiving the sacraments, singing sacred songs, or studying the Scriptures, we come actively to anticipate a fresh visitation of the Holy Spirit among us. The fostering of such a disposition is hard and slow work. In most cases, it will require a great deal of patience on the part of clergy and mature laity, as many churches have been taught to expect very little from God. As we have said before, clergy and lay leaders can do worse than to begin every service, every staff and committee meeting, and every gathering of the faithful with an acknowledgment of the presence of the Holy Spirit among us. In acknowledging the Holy Spirit, we should also give voice on behalf of the congregation to a ready willingness joyfully to listen for and to obey the Holy Spirit in all that we say and do together.

On the other hand, we must acquire wisdom and discernment in our use of the varied means of grace that the Holy Spirit makes available in the church. We must learn once again to be good catechists and spiritual directors, knowing when to add and when to take away, when to prescribe and when to guide, when to talk and when to listen. We need to think carefully about when to encourage people to read the Scriptures and when to encourage them to study the Creed. We must be able to discern when and how people are ready to confess their sins and when and how they are ready to receive forgiveness. Some of us may even need to apprentice ourselves to persons who truly know how to do this work, which is to say, to persons belonging to ecclesial traditions that take the practice of spiritual direction seriously (e.g., the Jesuits).

All things considered, this is good news. The Holy Spirit has not left us bereft of resources. On the contrary, the Spirit has blessed us with means of grace for our healing and our salvation. We need only to rediscover the resources that are literally at our fingertips and to learn how to use them wisely.

Perfect Ministry and Perfect Love: The Goal of Church Renewal

At the outset of this chapter, we suggested that it is vitally important to think carefully about the desired effects of church renewal. All too often, we do not get past the need to stave off further numeric decline and, if possible, to increase worship attendance and church membership. However, there is surely more to church renewal than this. After all, the world is not lacking for large crowds gathered together in one place.[40]

In the postmodern West, people want to know more than how big the church is. They want to know whether the church has anything of substance to offer. They want to know whether the Christian God is impotent or indifferent. They want to know whether Christians are truly different; whether we are the called-out ones, sanctified and made perfect in love for God and ministry to one another and to the world. They want to know whether the church is a place of spiritual stagnation or genuine spiritual growth.

To speak of perfect ministry and perfect love as the *goal* of church renewal will no doubt strike some as hopelessly optimistic and unrealistic. We must be very careful to say that by perfect ministry and perfect love we do not mean that the church should advertise herself as a sinless or flawless community. Rather, perfect ministry and perfect love is the goal toward which the church strains. Indispensable to this straining is the ongoing work of mutual confession, repentance, and forgiveness. Indeed, the church will be about the business of perfect ministry and perfect love only when she becomes the kind of place where people feel free to tell the truth about themselves. Far from a sign of imperfection, humble repentance and forgiveness is a crucial part of perfect ministry and perfect love made possible by the presence and work of the Holy Spirit among the people of God.

Having said these things, what ought to set the church apart from the wider culture in which it is situated is a robust sense that *we are not doomed perpetually to repeat our sins.* We are not doomed perpetually to violate ourselves and those around us. We are not doomed to self-hatred or pride, to manipulation or victimhood. We are not doomed to selfishness, to greed, or to lust. We are not doomed to racism, sexism, and ethnocentrism. Thus while the church must provide time and space for humble repentance and for forgiveness, she must also make clear that she possesses powerful medicine by which we can be delivered from our violence and insanity, from our hostilities and insecurities, and from all forms of idolatry. So equipped, what we ought to desire in our efforts to renew the church is nothing less than the sanctification and perfecting of the people of God.

The perfecting of the church in ministry and love is not an abstract idea without shape or content. On the contrary, perfect ministry and perfect love are concrete in their manifestation. The Spirit sanctifies and perfects the church in and through the means of grace which the Spirit so generously makes available. Through the means of grace, including prayer, repentance, confession, fasting, worship, reading the Scriptures, the sacraments, and the like, the Holy Spirit creates divine graces in the people of God that they would not otherwise enjoy and for which they would not otherwise have a capacity.

While the church has described the divine graces that the Holy Spirit creates in her members in a variety of ways across the centuries, three ways of talking about them are especially worth mentioning. In and through the sacramental life of the church, the Holy Spirit forms in the church's members (1) the mind of Christ, (2) the theological virtues, and (3) the fruits of the Spirit. Through the formation of the mind of Christ, the Holy Spirit enables the church's members to exhibit the attitudes and dispositions of a servant in their relationships to God, to one another, and to the world (Phil 2). Rather than clinging to their lives, the church's members are enabled by the Holy Spirit to give their lives away freely for the sake of others. Through the formation of the theological virtues, the Holy Spirit enables the church's members to exhibit faith, hope, and love in good times and bad (1 Cor 13). Instead of turning to cynicism and despair or to a politics of revenge, the Holy Spirit enables the church's members to remain faithful unto death, to give the hopeless reason to hope, and to embody a politics of loving kindness toward friends and enemies alike. In bringing about the fruits of the Spirit, the Holy Spirit enables the church's members truly to display love, joy, peace, patience, gentleness, goodness, kindness, and self-control toward one another and toward the world (Galatians 5).

When the mind of Christ, the theological virtues, and the fruits of the Spirit are manifest in the life of the church, people cannot help noticing. After all, life in the postmodern West is anything but loving and peaceful. As often as not, mainstream media in the postmodern West celebrate and promote revenge and violence over forgiveness and peace. Similarly, the workplace and the marketplace in the postmodern West are hardly known for patience and kindness. On the contrary, intemperance and rudeness are the order of the day. Likewise, the communities to which so many of us belong are often bereft of joy and thanksgiving.

The truth is that we do not need more demographic or generational studies to figure out what people are looking for. In the midst of workplaces full of resentment and hostility, people are searching for love. Surrounded by anxiety and depression, people are looking for joy. Amid the violence and insanity of city streets and war-torn countries, people are searching high and low for peace. Faced with spouses and co-workers who lose their tempers at a moment's notice, people are looking for self-control. Amid rampant road rage, people are in desperate need of patience. Against the backdrop that is the harshness and cruelty of the evening news, people will inevitably be drawn to churches that exhibit gentleness and kindness in every aspect of their lives. Over against the gospel of pervasive pessimism about human nature and human communities, people will be drawn to churches that proclaim and embody a gospel of transformation and holiness.

Conceived along these lines, the real question for the church is not whether we can get people to come to church in the first place. The real question is whether, upon coming, they will find compelling reasons to return time and time again. The deep contention of this book is that people will not be drawn to and held captive by the church simply because it carefully preserves and maintains its long-standing structures. Nor will they be drawn to and held captive by the church simply because it is part of a prophetic movement aimed at renewal or reform. Rather, people will ultimately be drawn to and held captive by the church when they discover in the church something they cannot readily get anywhere else, namely, a community that embodies in readily discernible ways the mind of Christ, the theological virtues, and the fruits of the Spirit.[41] In other words, they will be drawn to and held captive by those churches that bear the marks of incorporation into the Trinitarian life of God. Short of this, people may come to the church for a season, but they will ultimately look elsewhere for their salvation.

Conclusion

For if ever an age yearned for authentic sanctity,
surely it is ours.

—*Sarah Coakley*

Many proposals for church renewal begin by asking the question, "What is wrong with the church?" We deliberately avoided this strategy, beginning instead with the question, "What is the nature of the church?" We then proceeded to inquire about the mission of the church and the sacramental life of the church. In doing so, our goal has been to develop a theological framework within which to think about and to assess the many proposals for church renewal presently swirling around us.

Some renewal advocates will likely view our failure to begin by naming what is wrong with the church as the Achilles heel, if not the fatal flaw, in this project. We can readily anticipate the argument that will be made along these lines. It goes something like this. The problem with the Western church in the twenty-first century is that it is hopelessly out of touch with the culture around it. Over the years, we have been so utterly preoccupied with ourselves that we have failed to notice that many people are now either indifferent toward or openly hostile to the church. In other words, we have failed to notice that the West is now thoroughly secularized. Thus our entire project is actually part of the problem. Instead of working to develop strategies for overcoming people's indifference or hostility toward the church, we have simply undergone one more round of ecclesial navel-gazing. Instead of looking at the church through the window that is the eyes of the wider secular culture, we have once again been admiring ourselves in the mirror. In conclusion, we clearly need to respond to this objection.

While we did not begin by naming what is wrong with the Western church, we have been circling around a diagnosis. Indeed, the careful reader will have noticed that, throughout this work, we have been battling a strong undertow in our thinking about church renewal. To make explicit our diagnosis of what is wrong with the Western church, we must now name this undertow.

In our thinking about the nature, mission, and sacramental life of the church, we have had to ward off an entire host of distractions, including our preoccupation with the many shortcomings of the churches that we know and love, our determination to save ourselves, our concerns about acceptable forms for worship and witness, and our tendency to drive a wedge between the prophetic and the structural. All of these distractions have one thing in common: they take our focus off the One who is the source and end of our life, namely, the Holy Trinity. This is the undertow against which we have had to struggle in every chapter. This is also our diagnosis of what is wrong with the church. Whether we are hitching our wagons to prophetic leaders and movements or zealously defending ecclesial structures, we tend to leave God out of the equation. In other words, much of our discourse about what has gone wrong with the church and about how to put things right is functionally deistic.[1]

At this stage, someone is bound to object that our diagnosis of what is wrong with the church—that we persistently leave God out of the equation—does next to nothing to overcome the distance that has opened up between the church and the thoroughly secularized West. If anything, all our talk about the Trinity and about the sacramental life of the church will only serve further to alienate the church from those we should be trying to love and serve. Such talk may tickle the ears of the theologically high-minded among us, but it will come off as little more than meaningless babble to virtually everyone else.

Our response to this objection is simple and straightforward, if not uncontested.[2] Increasingly, there are good reasons to believe that the claim that the wider culture is thoroughly secular (i.e., indifferent or hostile toward religion) is significantly overblown. In other words, it is precisely those who view the culture as thoroughly secularized who are hopelessly out of step with the culture. To see this clearly, we need to identify and call into question the two assumptions behind the claim that the wider culture is thoroughly "secular."

The first assumption has to do with people's sensibilities about the whole of reality. Many church leaders today take it for granted that people are utterly skeptical about the supernatural. This assumption is part and parcel of what most clergy mean by "secular." In this view, secular people and cultures either disbelieve in the existence of God and other supernatural beings altogether, or they believe that, if supernatural beings exist, we cannot possibly know anything about them. Embedded in this assumption is a supporting assumption that people desire and value rationality or intellectual credibility above all else. Thus people are indifferent or hostile toward Christianity primarily because they regard belief in God, the incarnation, the resurrection, and the like, as irrational or otherwise lacking in intellectual credibility.

The interesting thing about the assumption that the culture is intellectually indifferent or hostile toward Christianity is that it has been so widely embraced by virtually all Protestants in the postmodern West. For example, it is easy to find both evangelicals and mainline liberals who subscribe to this assumption about Western culture. The difference between these groups is not the diagnosis but the response. For more than a century, leading evangelicals have expended an enormous amount of energy attempting to counter the perceived objection that Christianity is not rational or justifiable. As a result, we now have a vast apologetic literature that ranges from the popular to the academic, the sole purpose of which is to exonerate Christianity from charges of irrationality.[3] During this same period, many mainline liberal Protestants responded by downplaying or setting aside altogether the supernatural trappings of the Christian faith, focusing their message on social ethics instead. We now have a vast literature that exemplifies this strategy as well.[4]

The second assumption about the wider "secular" culture has to do with prevailing moral sensibilities. Many church leaders today assume that, when it comes to morality, the wider culture is utterly cynical and pessimistic. In other words, they assume that the culture finds any and all talk of moral goodness or sanctity preposterous and off-putting. Consequently, we routinely assure the culture that Christians do not think they are any different than non-Christians. We play down any talk of holiness or transformation for fear that such talk will meet with one big collective eye roll from a thoroughly skeptical culture. Indeed, we can readily see this move encapsulated in the popular Christian bumper stickers and tee-shirts that read, "Christians aren't perfect, just forgiven." In academic circles, the problem is even worse. To test this, we need only to mention the lives of the saints or the doctrines of sanctification and transfiguration at any number of sessions in the American Academy of Religion. Whether we are among self-described evangelical or liberal scholars, the mere mention of such things is likely to meet with either cynicism or laughter, or perhaps both.[5]

The problem with these two assumptions about the wider culture in the postmodern West is that they are increasingly outdated. To be sure, we could justifiably characterize a cross section of the wider culture in the *modern* West (most notably the intellectually elite) as indifferent or hostile toward religion in general and toward Christianity in particular. For example, we can readily discern a great deal of intellectual and moral skepticism about "organized religion" still emanating from the 1960s. But we now appear to be moving beyond this period of hyperskepticism. In fact, a genuine openness toward and growing interest in religion are two of the hallmarks of intellectual life in the postmodern West. Thus a growing number of studies suggests that interest in religion courses on college and university campuses is stronger than ever.[6] Similarly, in many metropolitan areas, Zen centers and Islamic mosques are full, and new religions are flourishing like never before. Moreover, books about religion are routinely at the top of the best-seller lists. Even the once secular news media are scrambling to cover noteworthy religious stories. As a result, a growing number of sociologists of religion are contending that secularism is now dead.[7] Indeed, for those with eyes to see, the postmodern West is teeming with religion.

There is also reason to think that we are now moving beyond a period of utter skepticism and pessimism about morality. For example, the eagerness with which Americans took to Barack Obama's rhetoric of hope, responsibility, and transformation suggests that the wider culture is ready to reengage in the quest for goodness and morality and to leave behind the old claims that racism and sexism, classism and ethnocentrism are insurmountable. Similarly, in the wake of much disappointment over the repeated moral failures of athletes, entertainers, politicians, and clergy, there is growing interest in stories of moral goodness and grace. Thus ESPN is just as likely to cover an athlete who gives generously of her time to the Special Olympics as to one who tests positive for steroids.[8]

Unfortunately, the church has been slow to perceive the changes in the wider culture's attitude toward religion and toward the quest for moral goodness. We have failed to see the growing openness toward and genuine interest in the supernatural, as well as the mounting desire for sanctity. The reasons we have failed to perceive these changes are many, but two are especially worth noting. First, in the 1960s, if not before, many mainline liberal Protestant churches utterly internalized an unholy trinity of skepticism, suspicion, and sarcasm with respect to both the cognitive contents and the moral claims of Christianity. Over the years, many of these churches and their leaders have become so mired in a hermeneutics of suspicion and in a radical form of skepticism that they simply cannot see that the world around them has once again begun to operate from a hermeneutics of trust and with epistemological humility and generosity with respect to religion. Many mainline liberal Protestants are so blinded by their bitterness and cynicism that they cannot see the brave new religious world that is opening up right in front of their eyes.

Second, many evangelical churches are still operating out of a predominantly defensive posture. Since the 1960s, if not before, evangelicals have been publicly ridiculed, mocked, and humiliated by intellectual and social elites in the mainstream media and in the wider culture in general. They have spent the last fifty years defending their beliefs and values. They are so accustomed to being attacked, that they cannot fathom a situation in which a question about their faith from an unbeliever might be something other than a setup. Consequently, many evangelical theologians and church leaders are now responding to questions that fewer and fewer people are asking and to charges that fewer and fewer people are levying. Like their liberal Protestant counterparts, they simply cannot see that a new situation is now breaking in upon them.

To make matters worse, many liberals and evangelicals are blinded to the shifts taking place around them precisely because they cannot take their eyes off one another long enough to take notice. It is as though evangelical and liberal Protestants are locked in a death embrace in which both sides are equally obsessed with killing one another.[9] All the while, we keep buried in our basements the solid food for which a spiritually hungry generation is searching far and wide.

If I am right about the changing sensibilities in the wider culture of the postmodern West, then we need to stop and ask ourselves whether it is time to adjust our strategies for reaching the culture around us. We need to ask ourselves whether first-time inquirers want to hear arguments in defense of the existence of God or self-flagellating apologies about the church's complicity in social and structural evil. This is not to say that there is not a time and a place for such things. It is simply to suggest that visitors may now be looking for something more basic and fundamental, namely, to hear what the Holy Trinity is like and to see what difference the Holy Trinity has made in the lives of Christians. It is to suggest that we may now be living in a time in which people are longing to encounter the sacred and in which they are searching high and low for the holy.

If this reading of the culture is even half right, then the time has come for the church to regain her confidence that she really does have a gift of inestimable value to offer to the world—something that the world cannot readily acquire elsewhere, namely, incorporation into the Trinitarian life of God. For better or worse, this is the only gift that the church has ever had to offer to the world. Accordingly, what ultimately matters with regard to prophetic movements and ecclesial structures is whether or not, with the help of the Holy Spirit, we can learn once again to receive and to appropriate them both not as ends in themselves, but as means of grace through which we can come to know and to love the Triune God. Whether or not the wider culture is ready to receive this gift is a matter that is open for debate. As we have noted, there is mounting evidence that it is. But even if we are wrong about the intellectual and moral sensibilities of the wider culture, the fact remains that this is the only gift that the church has to offer. And even this she does not really have. Rather, she receives it anew and afresh each day from the Holy Spirit. Therein is the source of our hope for the future.

Notes

INTRODUCTION

1 E. R. Dodds, *Pagan and Christian in an Age of Anxiety* (Cambridge: Cambridge University Press, 1965).

2 Dodds, *Pagan and Christian*, 103–4. He is here describing the first full century of Christian history.

3 Dodds, *Pagan and Christian*, 66.

4 Dodds, *Pagan and Christian*, 67–68.

5 By prophecy, I do not have in mind the practice of predicting the future. Rather, I have in mind the longstanding practice within Judaism and Christianity of daring to call the people of God to repent, to return to God, and to follow God in some new direction or venture. Of course, such calls can have a predictive element insofar as prophets sometimes warn the people of God that they will not flourish again if they do not repent, return to God, and follow God wherever God is leading, but they do not generally involve predictions of specific future events.

6 We can even see this in the history of ancient Israel as conveyed in the Old Testament. Thus Thomas B. Dozeman has recently highlighted the tension between the prophetic and the priestly with respect to the work of ministry in general and the cultivation of holiness in particular in ancient Israel. See his *Holiness and Ministry: A Biblical Theology of Ordination* (New York: Oxford University Press, 2008).

7 Like Montanus before them, Francis of Assisi, Martin Luther, and John Wesley were all critics of the church's leadership. Also like Montanus, they all encountered the concern for structure and the drive for order.

8   E.g., see Jaroslav Pelikan's little known but masterful work, *Spirit versus Structure: Luther and the Institutions of the Church* (New York: Harper & Row, 1968). On the tensions between John Wesley and the structures of the Church of England, see my *Wesley: A Guide for the Perplexed* (London: T&T Clark, 2009), chaps. 1–2.

9   The focus of this work is the church in North America and in western Europe. These are the contexts that I will have in mind when I talk about the Western church or the church in the postmodern West. Also, I am thinking primarily of evangelical and liberal Protestant churches, though I suspect that Roman Catholic and Eastern Orthodox churches are facing similar pressures. Finally, while the majority of the examples derive from churches and denominations in the United States of America, many of the issues highlighted by those examples are also prevalent in western European countries.

10 The work of the mid-twentieth-century Roman Catholic theologian Yves Congar is crucial here, especially his *I Believe in the Holy Spirit* (New York: Crossroad, 1999), vol. 2, pt. 1. For more on Congar, I recommend Elizabeth Groppe's *Yves Congar's Theology of the Holy Spirit* (New York: Oxford University Press, 2004), and Douglas M. Koskela's *Ecclesiality and Ecumenism: Yves Congar and the Road to Unity* (Milwaukee, Wis.: Marquette University Press, 2008).

11 For more on this, see *Canonical Theism: A Proposal for Theology and the Church*, edited by William J. Abraham, Jason E. Vickers, and Natalie B. Van Kirk (Grand Rapids: Eerdmans, 2008). Also see *Immersed in the Life of God: The Healing Practices of the Christian Faith*, edited by Paul L. Gavrilyuk, Douglas M. Koskela, and Jason E. Vickers (Grand Rapids: Eerdmans, 2008).

12 E.g., in mainline Protestant denominations, many are openly questioning whether or not the large boards and agencies that served the church well in the mid-twentieth century are now hindering the church in the early twenty-first century. Some are issuing open calls for the downsizing or even elimination of such boards and agencies. See Andy Langford and William H. Willimon, *A New Connection: Reforming the United Methodist Church* (Nashville, Tenn.: Abingdon, 1996).

13 R. R. Reno, *In the Ruins of the Church: Sustaining Faith in an Age of Diminished Christianity* (Grand Rapids: Brazos, 2002). For Reno, the Episcopal Church in particular was increasingly in ruins. In this book, he proposed that Episcopalians remain faithful amid the turmoil and division over homosexuality. Soon after the book was published, Reno left the Anglican fold for the Roman Catholic Church. See R. R. Reno, "Out of the Ruins," *First Things* 150 (2005): 11–16.

14 Ephraim Radner, *The End of the Church: A Pneumatology of Christian Division in the West* (Grand Rapids: Eerdmans, 1998). As the subtitle suggests, Radner is attempting to take seriously the reality of church division.

15 While not a theologian, Alasdair MacIntyre has been deeply influential on

many North American theologians. For his forecasting of a new dark age, see *After Virtue*, 3rd ed. (Notre Dame, Ind.: University of Notre Dame Press, 2007).

16 Mike Regele, *The Death of the Church* (Grand Rapids: Zondervan, 1996).

17 Julia Duin, *Quitting Church: Why the Faithful Are Fleeing and What to Do about It* (Grand Rapids: Baker Books, 2009).

18 David Murrow, *Why Men Hate Going to Church* (Waco, Tex.: Thomas Nelson, 2004).

19 Brian McClaren, *Finding Our Way Again: The Return of the Ancient Practices* (Waco, Tex.: Thomas Nelson, 2008).

20 There is now a vast literature on this. For statistics related to decline and a vivid picture of the overall situation in both western Europe and North America, see Philip Jenkins, *The Next Christendom: The Coming of Global Christianity*, rev. ed. (New York: Oxford University Press, 2007). Also, a wealth of studies on the decline of Western churches can be found at the Pew Forum on Religion and Public Life's website: http://pewforum.org.

21 David Martin, *Pentecostalism: The World Their Parish* (Boston: Blackwell, 2001).

22 As an ordained elder and seminary professor, I routinely accept invitations to preach in my students' churches, the vast majority of which are congregations in steep decline. Before and after worship services, I make a point of talking with the faithful, inquiring about the history of the church, about their memories, and the like. With a little prompting, I have found them eager to tell about the days when their churches were truly thriving.

23 I am not suggesting that individual improprieties are not sinful or immoral. Rather, I am simply distinguishing between the sinful activities of a pastor or priest that other clergy and church leaders do not know about, and the sinful activities of a pastor or priest that are known by other clergy and church leaders and yet remain undisclosed to the wider church community or the public.

24 See David Kinnaman, *unChristian: What a New Generation Really Thinks about Christianity . . . and Why It Matters* (Grand Rapids: Baker Books, 2007), chap. 3.

25 For an early but still important examination of these disputes, see Nancy T. Ammerman, *Baptist Battles: Social Change and Religious Conflict in the Southern Baptist Convention* (Piscataway, N.J.: Rutgers University Press, 1990).

26 For a recent work that foregrounds the death of Christendom in the West, see Bryan Stone, *Evangelism after Christendom: The Theology and Practice of Christian Witness* (Grand Rapids: Brazos, 2007). For an older but still important work, see Stanley Hauerwas, *After Christendom: How the Church Is to Behave if Freedom, Justice, and a Christian Nation Are Bad Ideas* (Nashville, Tenn.: Abingdon, 1991). For a thorough critique of Hauerwas' position, see Nicholas Wolterstorff, *Justice: Rights and Wrongs* (Princeton, N.J.: Princeton University Press, 2010).

27   For a landmark and now classic work on this topic, see Stanley Hauerwas and William H. Willimon, *Resident Aliens: Life in the Christian Colony* (Nashville, Tenn.: Abingdon, 1989).

28   In the conclusion to this work, we will suggest that the secularization thesis, and with it the post-Christendom thesis, has been greatly overblown. Far from antireligious, we will maintain that the postmodern West is hyperreligious.

29   For all the fuss over the so-called "new atheism," I am convinced that atheism has never been a widespread problem in the West. On balance, westerners are intensely religious. We will invent new gods before we will abandon theism altogether. For more on the "new atheism," see John F. Haught, *God and the New Atheism: A Critical Response to Dawkins, Harris, and Hitchens* (Louisville, Ky.: Westminster John Knox, 2007). For a work that uses demographic and other statistical studies to demonstrate that Americans in particular are deeply religious, see Rodney Stark, *What Americans Really Believe* (Waco, Tex.: Baylor University Press, 2008).

30   For a classic work on this aspect of Western culture in the late twentieth century, see Neil Postman, *Amusing Ourselves to Death: Public Discourse in the Age of Show Business*, 20th anniv. ed. (New York: Penguin, 2005). Also see Robert N. Bellah et al., *Habits of the Heart: Individualism and Commitment in American Life*, 3rd ed. (Berkeley: University of California Press, 2007).

31   In an innovative and bold move, a United Methodist Church in Anderson, Indiana, tried to entice young families to come to church by hosting a soccer league on Sundays. Unfortunately, the move does not appear to have been highly successful. For more on this, see Heather Hahn, "Soccer Sundays: How Do Churches Compete?" The People of the United Methodist Church website, July 2, 2010, http://www.umc.org/site/apps/nlnet/content3.aspx?c=lwL4KnN1LtH&b=5259669&ct=8493205 (accessed July 5, 2010).

32   E.g., the Claremont School of Theology's decision to develop an approach to theological education that is religiously pluralist has sparked a lively debate within the United Methodist Church concerning the evangelization of persons of other faith traditions. See Robin Russell, "Claremont's Religious Diversity: Church Affirms Multi-Faith Project," *United Methodist Reporter*, July 2, 2010, http://www.umportal.org/article.asp?id=6914 (accessed August 18, 2010).

33   Scores of studies are available on this topic. E.g., see Thomas Frejka and Jean-Paul Sardon, *Childbearing Trends and Prospects in Low-Fertility Countries: A Cohort Analysis* (Dordrecht: Kluwer Academic, 2004). Also see Russell Shorto, "No Babies?" in *The New York Times*, June 29, 2008, http://www.nytimes.com/2008/06/29/magazine/29Birth-t.html (accessed July 7, 2010).

34   For the professionalization of the ministry, see E. Brooks Holifield, *God's Ambassadors: A History of the Christian Clergy in America* (Grand Rapids: Eerdmans, 2007).

35 This is one of the more important insights to be gleaned from liberation theologies.

36 Many of the founders of university-based divinity schools in America dreamed of dominating intellectual life. They believed that divinity schools would be at the center of a grand Protestant project that would eventuate in the perfecting of Western culture. For more on this, see Conrad Cherry, *Hurrying toward Zion: Universities, Divinity Schools, and American Protestantism* (Bloomington: Indiana University Press, 1995).

37 E.g., see Daniel O. Aleshire, *Earthen Vessels: Hopeful Reflection on the Work and Future of Theological Schools* (Grand Rapids: Eerdmans, 2008).

38 The crucial work on this is Stephen Prothero, *Religious Literacy: What Every American Needs to Know—and Doesn't* (New York: HarperOne, 2008).

39 For the history of this shift, see Randy L. Maddox, "Recovery of Theology as a Practical Discipline: A Contemporary Agenda," *Theological Studies* 51 (1990): 650–72. Fortunately, many theologians today are hard at work restoring the connection between theology and worship. E.g., see *A More Profound Alleluia: Theology and Worship in Harmony*, edited by Leanne Van Dyk (Grand Rapids: Eerdmans, 2004).

40 Donald A. McGavran and C. Peter Wagner, *Understanding Church Growth*, 3rd ed. (Grand Rapids: Eerdmans, 1990).

41 Rick Warren, *The Purpose Driven Church* (Grand Rapids: Zondervan, 1995).

42 Darrell Guder, *Missional Church: A Vision for the Sending of the Church in North America* (Grand Rapids: Eerdmans, 1998); Alan Hirsch, *The Forgotten Ways: Reactivating the Missional Church* (Grand Rapids: Brazos, 2007); and Mike Slaughter, *Change the World: Recovering the Message and Mission of Jesus* (Nashville, Tenn.: Abingdon, 2010).

43 Ray S. Anderson, *An Emergent Theology for Emergent Churches* (Downers Grove, Ill.: InterVarsity, 2006); Tony Jones, *The New Christians: Dispatches from the Emergent Frontier* (San Francisco: Jossey-Bass, 2008); and Dan Kimball, *The Emerging Church: Vintage Christianity for New Generations* (Grand Rapids: Zondervan, 2003).

44 Shane Claiborne, *The Irresistible Revolution: Living as an Ordinary Radical* (Grand Rapids: Zondervan, 2006); Jonathan Wilson-Hartgrove, *New Monasticism: What It Has to Say to Today's Church* (Grand Rapids: Brazos, 2008); and Elaine Heath, *The Mystic Way of Evangelism: A Contemplative Vision for Christian Outreach* (Grand Rapids: Baker Academic, 2008).

45 Robert Webber, *Ancient-Future Faith: Rethinking Evangelicalism for a Postmodern World* (Grand Rapids: Baker Academic, 1999). Also see Webber's books on ancient-future worship, ancient-future evangelism, and ancient-future time.

46 Neil Cole, *Organic Church: Growing Faith Where Life Happens* (San Francisco: Jossey-Bass, 2005); and Frank Viola, *Finding Organic Church: A Comprehensive Guide to Starting and Sustaining Authentic Christian Communities* (Colorado Springs: David C. Cook, 2009).

47 Pete Ward, *Liquid Church* (Peabody, Mass.: Hendrickson, 2002).

48 Larry Osborne, *Sticky Church* (Grand Rapids: Zondervan, 2008).

49 Carol Merritt, *Tribal Church: Ministering to the Missing Generation* (Herndon, Va.: Alban Institute, 2007).

50 Jim Belcher, *Deep Church: A Third Way beyond Emerging and Traditional* (Downers Grove, Ill.: InterVarsity, 2009).

51 E.g., in my own area, Mike Slaughter, a nationally known leader in the missional church movement and senior pastor of Ginghamsburg United Methodist Church, hosts an annual Change the World conference that routinely features renewalists like Brian McClaren and Alan Hirsch as keynote speakers. The conference is extremely popular with clergy from across a wide spectrum of denominations.

52 For more on intradenominational renewal groups, see Thomas C. Oden, *Turning Around the Mainline: How Renewal Movements Are Changing the Church* (Grand Rapids: Baker Books, 2006).

53 See Thomas G. Long, *Beyond the Worship Wars: Building Vital and Faithful Worship* (Herndon, Va.: The Alban Institute, 2001).

54 While large churches have strengths, we need to pay more attention to the unique strengths and contributions of small churches. On this front, I heartily recommend Jason Byassee's *The Gifts of the Small Church* (Nashville, Tenn.: Abingdon, 2010).

55 They are not the primary reason to be hopeful. As I will argue in the concluding chapter of this work, the primary reason for hope is what it has always been, namely, the presence and work of the Holy Spirit, and therefore of the Holy Trinity, in our midst.

56 This is certainly true of today's prophetic leaders and movements. E.g., the missional church movement is intensely focused on helping the church to recover a heart and a passion for serving the needs of the world.

57 I will sometimes talk about the church's materials, persons, and practices. This handy typology originated with William J. Abraham's *Canon and Criterion in Christian Theology: From the Fathers to Feminism* (Oxford: Oxford University Press, 1998).

58 I take it for granted that so-called independent or nondenominational churches are no less situated in particular theological traditions than denominational churches.

59 E.g., Sergius Bulgakov's *The Bride of the Lamb* (Grand Rapids: Eerdmans, 2002) and Nicholas Afansiev's *The Church of the Holy Spirit* (Notre Dame, Ind.: University of Notre Dame Press, 2007) are clearly embedded in the Eastern Orthodox tradition, whereas Radner's *The End of the Church* and Reno's *In the Ruins of the Church* bear the marks of the Anglican tradition.

60 I have written more extensively and more explicitly elsewhere on each of these aspects of my theological and ecclesial tradition. For more on the pneumatological orientation of John and Charles Wesley's theology, see my

"Wesley's Theological Emphases," in *The Cambridge Companion to John Wesley*, edited by Randy L. Maddox and Jason E. Vickers (New York: Cambridge University Press, 2010), 190–206. Also see my "Charles Wesley's Doctrine of the Holy Spirit: A Vital Resource for the Renewal of Methodism," *Asbury Theological Journal* 61, no. 1 (2006): 47–60. For more on the pietist and revivalist heritage of Methodism with a view toward the renewal of Methodism today, see *Methodist and Pietist: Retrieving the EUB Heritage*, edited by J. Steven O'Malley and Jason E. Vickers (Nashville, Tenn.: Kingswood Books, 2011). For more on evangelism and conversion, see my "To Know and to Love God Truly: The Healing Power of Conversion," in *Immersed in the Life of God: The Healing Resources of the Christian Faith*, edited by Paul L. Gavrilyuk, Douglas M. Koskela, and Jason E. Vickers (Grand Rapids: Eerdmans, 2008), 1–20. For more on the twin concern for personal and social holiness, see my "Albert Outler and the Future of Wesleyan Theology: Retrospect and Prospect," in *Wesleyan Theological Journal* 42, no. 2 (2008): 56–67.

61 World Council of Churches, *The Nature and Mission of the Church: A Stage on the Way to a Common Statement* (Geneva: The World Council of Churches, 2005) (hereafter cited as *NMC*).

CHAPTER 1

1 The discipline of ecclesiology has to do with critical reflection on the doctrine of the church (emphasis in original).

2 For a substantial work on the offices of ministry, see Afansiev, *The Church of the Holy Spirit*. Protestants in particular should read this work most carefully.

3 It is interesting to note that, in the letters to the seven churches in Revelation, some of the harshest consequences are reserved for the Laodicean church, which is to say, for the church that had become indifferent. For an excellent work on church renewal that enters into critical and creative conversation with the letters to the churches in Revelation, see T. Scott Daniels, *Seven Deadly Spirits: The Message of Revelation's Letters for Today's Church* (Grand Rapids: Baker Academic, 2009).

4 We will have more to say about this in the conclusion to this chapter. For now, suffice it to say that, in an age of anxiety, the way to begin doing ecclesiology is not by grabbing a megaphone but by becoming still, even silent, before God.

5 Slaughter, *Change the World*, 31.

6 For more on this theme, I recommend the work of Sarah Coakley. E.g., on the Spirit's work of incorporation into the Trinitarian life of God, see Sarah Coakley, "Why Three? Some Further Reflections on the Origins of the Doctrine of the Trinity," in *The Making and Remaking of Christian Doctrine: Essays in Honour of Maurice Wiles*, edited by Sarah Coakley and David A. Pailin (Oxford: Oxford University Press, 1993), 29–56.

7   Thus people who are thinking about acquiring a dog routinely purchase books that list the distinguishing features of the most popular breeds.

8   Long neglected in modern theology, ecumenical creeds and confessions of faith have made a strong comeback in recent years. Most notably, a growing number of historians, theologians, and even biblical scholars are making a case for the importance of the Nicene Creed for theological reflection. Especially worth noting on this front is the work of Rowan Greer, Luke Timothy Johnson, Jaroslav Pelikan, and Frances Young, to name a few.

9   Some readers will wonder why I do not simply advocate turning directly and perhaps exclusively to Scripture. The short answer to this question is that I do not subscribe to a wooden and literal interpretation of the doctrine of *sola scriptura*. Rather, I think that we should read and understand Scripture in light of rules or confessions of faith. With regard to the relationship between Scripture and the ecumenical creeds, I am especially sympathetic with the work of William J. Abraham, Craig Allert, Paul Gavrilyuk, David Yeago, and N. T. Wright. Contrary to the Troeltschian thesis that the ecumenical creeds somehow constitute a departure from Scripture, these authors maintain (and I agree) that the ecumenical creeds reflect a baptismal and theological grammar that emerged alongside and that inheres in Holy Scripture. For more on this, see especially David Yeago, "The New Testament and the Nicene Dogma: A Contribution to the Recovery of Theological Exegesis," *Sewanee Theological Review* 45, no. 4 (2002): 371–84.

10 It is interesting that the four marks are not separated by commas in the Nicene Creed. This would appear to suggest that these attributes are mutually interdependent. In other words, holiness catholicity and apostolicity are essential to oneness, oneness is essential to holiness catholicity and apostolicity, and so on. It is as though one must think of all four marks at once in order to think of any one of them rightly. I will say more about this when I return to the marks of the church in chapter 3.

11 For more on the biblical images for the church, see especially Paul S. Minear, *Images of the Church in the New Testament* (Cambridge: Lutterworth, 2007). Also see *NMC*, 6–8.

12 For more on the nature of metaphor, see Janet Martin Soskice, *Metaphor and Religious Language* (Oxford: Oxford University Press, 1987).

13 The marks of the church in the Nicene Creed and the Protestant confessions are no less subject to interpretation. E.g., the history of Christian theology has witnessed more than a few disagreements over the content of the "pure word of God" or the meaning of holiness, catholicity, and apostolicity. Indeed, one way to understand the ecumenical movement of the late twentieth and early twenty-first centuries is to see it as a movement in which church leaders and theologians are attempting to

overcome long-standing disagreements about the basis of church unity, the meaning of catholicity, the location of apostolicity, and so forth. Far from consensus, what we have at the level of the World Council of Churches is a vital conversation about the meaning of the marks of the church in the Nicene Creed. See especially, World Council of Churches, *Confessing the One Faith: An Ecumenical Explication of the Apostolic Faith as It Is Confessed in the Nicene-Constantinopolitan Creed*, rev. ed. (Eugene, Ore.: Wipf and Stock, 2010).

14　To anticipate the argument ahead, I am suggesting here that, regardless of how we finesse the meaning of the terms, our *initial* judgment will be the same, namely, that the terms do not adequately describe the church as we know it. E.g., suppose we try out several different ways of defining holiness. My contention is that, in each case, we could make a good argument that the term does not adequately describe the church either synchronically or diachronically. In other words, in and through time, the church will be less than holy, regardless of how we define the term. However, as we will see up ahead, there is another way to think about this issue so that we really can predicate things like the holiness of the church. When we get to that stage in the argument, the same point will hold. No matter which definition we substitute for, say, holiness, we will be able to say that the church really is holy.

15　To see this clearly, imagine the following scenario. A person acquires a dog based on the distinguishing features of the breed listed in any number of authoritative manuals on dog breeds. After six months, the person is exasperated. The dog exhibits the opposite traits of the ones listed in the manual. So the person assumes that she must have acquired a "bad dog." She reasons that the manuals cannot be this far off in their descriptions. So she acquires another dog of the same breed only to suffer through the same process. Suppose she is determined to find an example of the breed that fits the descriptions in the manual. Thus she acquires six more dogs of the same breed, meeting with the same unhappy results every time. At some point, she would surely be justified if she were to conclude that the manuals were wrong about the nature of that particular breed of dog.

16　Hughes Oliphant Old, "Why Bother with Church?" in *Essentials of Christian Theology*, edited by William C. Placher (Louisville, Ky.: Westminster John Knox, 2003), 239.

17　The very existence of the ecumenical movement bears witness to this fact.

18　For a helpful discussion of whether Catholic and Orthodox claims to be the church identified by the Creed necessarily deny all legitimacy to other churches, see Geoffrey Wainwright, "Were Methodists Present at Constantinople 381? Ecclesial Claims in the Light of the Four Notes of the Conciliar Creed," in *Orthodox and Wesleyan Ecclesiology*, edited by S.

T. Kimbrough Jr. (Crestwood, N.Y.: St. Vladimir's Seminary Press, 2007), 21–41. Note especially Wainwright's discussion of the Russian statement of 2000 beginning on page 36.

19 For a theologically rich account of holiness, see John Webster, *Holiness* (Grand Rapids: Eerdmans, 2003).

20 For an attempt to maintain the church's holiness while acknowledging the sinfulness of her members, see John Paul II, "Post-Synodal Apostolic Exhortation of John Paul II to the Bishops, Clergy, and Faithful on Reconciliation and Penance in the Mission of the Church Today," Saint Peter's, Rome, December 2, 1984, sec. 16, www.vatican.va/holy_father/john_paul_ii/apost_exhortations/documents/hf_jp-ii_exh_02121984_reconciliatio-et-paenitentia_en.html (accessed August 12, 2010).

21 The problem of how to account for both continuity and development of doctrine across the centuries is a notorious one in theology. The best effort to solve the problem remains John Henry Newman's *An Essay on the Development of Christian Doctrine* (Notre Dame, Ind.: University of Notre Dame Press, 1989). Newman's proposal, while fascinating and enduring, is not without its problems. For a more recent well-known attempt to grapple with the issues at stake, see George Lindbeck, *The Nature of Doctrine: Religion and Theology in a Postliberal Age* (Philadelphia: Westminster, 1984). As with Newman's, Lindbeck's proposals are not problem-free. For some of the problems with Lindbeck's approach, see Alister McGrath, *The Genesis of Doctrine: A Study in the Foundation of Doctrinal Criticism* (Grand Rapids: Eerdmans, 1990).

22 Three standard examples include the church's complicity in the slave trade, in the oppression of women, and in the Nazi Holocaust.

23 The worst case here is clearly the present and growing crisis over pedophile priests in the Roman Catholic Church.

24 In chapter 3, I will suggest that this has been the besetting sin in many mainline Protestants churches in the late twentieth century.

25 For a discussion of some of the issues at stake and an interesting proposal for how Christians ought to think about the issues, see Bruce D. Marshall, "Christ and the Cultures: The Jewish People and Christian Theology," in *The Cambridge Companion to Christian Doctrine*, edited by Colin E. Gunton (New York: Cambridge University Press, 1997), 81–100.

26 Another possibility for understanding the nature of the church can be found in the Orthodox theologian Bulgakov's intriguing suggestion that, rightly understood, the church is eternal. Thus is does not make sense to speak of the beginning of the church. As I see it, it is possible to take Bulgakov's claim about the eternality of the church seriously and still speak of Pentecost as in a very real sense marking the beginning of the church as a new reality on earth. For the notion that the church is eternal, see Bulgakov, *Bride of the Lamb*, chap. 5.

27 I have in mind inquiries about the person and work of the Holy Spirit that proceed from a thoroughly skeptical point of view. By contrast, it is utterly refreshing that Christian philosophers are beginning to mine Pentecost and Pentecostal theology and spirituality for insights into ontology, epistemology, aesthetics, and the philosophy of language. On this front, see especially James K. A. Smith, *Thinking in Tongues: Pentecostal Contributions to Christian Philosophy* (Grand Rapids: Eerdmans, 2010).

28 For the Holy Spirit in the life of Jesus, see Raneiro Cantalamessa, *The Holy Spirit in the Life of Jesus* (Collegeville, Minn.: The Liturgical Press, 1994).

29 *NMC*, 4.

30 For more on the earliest days of the church, see especially Martin Hengel, *Between Jesus and Paul: Studies in the History of Earliest Christianity* (Eugene, Ore.: Wipf and Stock, 2003).

31 Irenaeus, "Against Heresies," in *The Ante-Nicene Fathers*, vol. 1, edited by Rev. Alexander Roberts, Sir James Donaldson, and Arthur Cleveland Coke (New York: Cosimo Classics, 2007), 3.24.1 (emphasis added).

32 *NMC*, 5 (emphasis added).

33 Bruno Forte, *The Church: Icon of the Trinity* (Toronto: Pauline Books, 1991).

34 See Miroslav Volf, *After Our Likeness: The Church as the Image of the Trinity* (Grand Rapids: Eerdmans, 1998), 191–220.

35 *NMC*, 12 (emphasis added).

36 At times, in an effort to acknowledge the reality of sin in the church and throughout the church's history, *NMC* can come close to this view. My own view is that the document fails to balance its robust account of the negative consequences of sin with an equally robust account of what is possible through grace.

37 For more on this way of understanding the work of the Spirit in the life of the church, see the essays in Gavrilyuk et al., *Immersed in the Life of God*.

38 This is a fictitious church name.

39 Readers from other traditions should feel free to substitute the terms that they use to talk about the structures that make up their systems.

40 The truth is that ecclesial structures began to emerge soon after Pentecost. E.g., see Francis Sullivan, *From Apostles to Bishops: The Development of the Episcopacy in the Early Church* (Mahwah, N.J.: Paulist, 2001).

41 Sarah Coakley, "The Vicar at Prayer: An English Reflection on Ministry," *Christian Century* 125, no. 13 (2008): 29. I highly recommend this article to seminary students preparing for ministry. It is electric reading! E.g., Coakley observes that most church advertisements for new ministers seek "a minister who is gifted in 'leadership' or one who is 'energetic' and 'efficient.' Rarely do they ask for one who is 'prayerful' (would this be regarded as precious or elitist?). This ecclesiastical trend toward secular models of personal efficacy is odd; for if ever an age yearned for authentic sanctity, surely it is ours" (28).

42 I do not intend here to suggest a manna vision of the work of the Holy
    Spirit. There is a real sense in which the Holy Spirit is ever present among
    us. Consequently, one could say that it does not make good sense to ask
    the Spirit to come. On the contrary, asking the Spirit to come is a way
    of recognizing the sheer gratuity of the Spirit's presence and our utter
    dependence on that gratuity. It is also to avoid a more dangerous prob-
    lem, namely, taking the Spirit's abiding presence among us for granted.
43 Richard John Neuhaus, *Death on a Friday Afternoon* (New York: Basic Books,
    2000), 90.

CHAPTER 2

1   See Ludwig Wittgenstein, *Philosophical Investigations*, 3rd ed., translated by
    G. E. M Anscombe (New York: Macmillan, 1953), 219.
2   A great example of the danger here can be seen in churches that self-iden-
    tify as "missional." Thus, while I deeply admire Mike Slaughter's work at
    Ginghamsburg United Methodist Church, I begin to get concerned when
    he talks about a "theology of sweat," about demanding a lot from church
    members, and the like. On the one hand, I share his commitment to hard
    work. On the other hand, we must be careful not to deceive ourselves into
    thinking that success in ministry is primarily a result of our labor. To be
    sure, we do not have to drive a wedge between our willingness to work
    hard and the work of the Holy Spirit. We simply must be careful not to
    overemphasize the role that *we* play in the work of ministry to such an
    extent that we neglect to place equal, if not more, stress on the work of
    the Holy Spirit *in and through us*. See Michael Slaughter, *Unlearning Church*
    (Nashville, Tenn.: Abingdon, 2008), chap. 10.
3   This is often referred to as the *missio Dei* or mission of God.
4   Jürgen Moltmann, *The Church in the Power of the Spirit*, translated by Marga-
    ret Kohl (Minneapolis: Fortress, 1993), 64.
5   *NMC*, 10.
6   *NMC*, 11.
7   See William H. Willimon, *Who Will Be Saved?* (Nashville, Tenn.: Abingdon,
    2009). Willimon seeks to expose the myth of self-sufficiency precisely
    where it is most hidden, namely, in the Christian doctrine of salvation.
8   No one has made this point more compellingly than Sarah Coakley. E.g.,
    see her "Living into the Mystery of the Holy Trinity: Trinity, Prayer, and
    Sexuality," *Anglican Theological Review* 80, no. 2 (1998): 223–32.
9   Karl Barth, *Prayer*, translated by Sara F. Terrien (Philadelphia: Westmin-
    ster, 1952), 20.
10 We will attend to the resources that the Holy Spirit has given to the
    church more fully in chapter 3.
11 *NMC* goes on to say, "Aware of God's saving presence in the world, the
    Church already praises and glorifies the Triune God through worship and

discipleship, and serves God's plan. Yet the Church does so not only for itself, but rather renders praise and thanks on behalf of all peoples for God's grace and the forgiveness of sins" (10–11).

12 *NMC*, 10.

13 *NMC*, 10.

14 *NMC*, 10. "As Christ's mission encompassed the preaching of the Word of God and the commitment to care for those in suffering and in need, so the apostolic Church in its mission from the beginning combined preaching of the word, the call to repentance, faith, baptism, and diakonia."

15 *NMC*, 10. "In the power of the Holy Spirit the Church testifies to the divine mission in which the Father sent the Son to be the Savior of the World."

16 For this way of viewing the wider culture in the United States, see Mark Bauerlein, *The Dumbest Generation: How the Digital Age Stupefies Young Americans and Jeopardizes Our Future (Or, Don't Trust Anyone under 30)* (Los Angeles: Tarcher, 2009).

17 A great example of this can be seen in the Church of the Nazarene. At the time of this writing, the Church of the Nazarene is divided over the emerging church to the point that they are discussing the matters at the highest levels of church government, namely, the level of the Board of General Superintendents and of General Assembly. For an example of the hostile opposition toward emerging worship, see the group "Concerned Nazarenes," whose self-proclaimed mission is to expose "the emergent church and contemplative spirituality that is infiltrating the denomination." See www.concernednazarenes.org (accessed June 23, 2010).

18 Robert Webber's work on the history of Christian worship is helpful here. Also see *The Oxford History of Christian Worship*, edited by Geoffrey Wainwright and Karen B. Westerfield Tucker (New York: Oxford University Press, 2005).

19 E.g., see Jaroslav Pelikan, *The Illustrated Jesus through the Centuries* (New Haven: Yale University Press, 1997).

20 For an arresting look at the places in which the vast majority of today's Christians worship, see especially Camilo Vergara, *How the Other Half Worships* (New Brunswick, N.J.: Rutgers University Press, 2005).

21 See my emphasis on the creativity and freedom of the Holy Spirit in Vickers, "Medicine of the Holy Spirit," 11–26.

22 H. Richard Niebuhr, *Faith on Earth: An Inquiry into the Structure of Human Faith* (New Haven: Yale University Press, 1991), 66.

23 It is interesting to note that, in the introduction to the original Methodist hymnbook, John Wesley spent a good deal of time talking about appropriate dispositions for worship!

24 See Vickers, "Medicine of the Holy Spirit," 11–26.

25 E.g., see Kimball, *The Emerging Church*.

26 It is not impossible for materials derived from popular culture to function

as symbols and sacraments that point beyond themselves to God. On the contrary, highly skilled liturgists and preachers can deploy resources from popular culture in such a way that the resources are transformed from mere signs to symbols. When this happens, it is often quite powerful, leaving impressions that literally last for a lifetime. Unfortunately, the ability to make highly effective use of resources gathered in from popular culture is one that most of us do not share. Indeed, we may have here to do with a special *charism* of the Holy Spirit in the life of the church.

27 Moltmann, *The Church in the Power of the Spirit*, 64.

28 See Cantalamessa, *The Holy Spirit in the Life of Jesus*.

29 This has certainly been the case historically. E.g., see Donald W. Dayton's work on the social activism of evangelical and holiness churches in *Discovering an Evangelical Heritage* (Peabody, Mass.: Hendrickson, 1988).

30 For helpful insights on the relationship between liberal or progressive Protestants and evangelical Protestants, see Christopher H. Evans, *Liberalism without Illusions: Renewing an American Christian Tradition* (Waco, Tex.: Baylor University Press, 2010).

31 For a helpful introduction to the main lines of interpretation and disagreement over the person and work of Christ, see Alan Spence, *Christology: A Guide for the Perplexed* (London: T&T Clark, 2008). Also see Tyron Inbody, *The Many Faces of Christology* (Nashville, Tenn.: Abingdon, 2002).

32 For these alternatives, see especially Marcus J. Borg and N. T. Wright, *The Meaning of Jesus: Two Visions* (New York: HarperOne, 2000). Also see C. Stephen Evans, *The Historical Christ and the Jesus of Faith: The Incarnational Narrative as History* (New York: Oxford University Press, 1996).

33 J. Denny Weaver, *The Non-Violent Atonement* (Grand Rapids: Eerdmans, 2001). For a contrasting view, see Andrew Sung Park, *Triune Atonement: Christ's Healing for Sinners, Victims, and the Whole Creation* (Louisville, Ky.: Westminster John Knox, 2009).

34 See Philip Jenkins, *Jesus Wars* (New York: HarperOne, 2010).

35 A great deal of harm has been done across the centuries when the church has, in her preaching and evangelism, failed to emphasize both the divine and human natures of Jesus Christ.

36 On contemplative ways of bearing witness in the Christian mystical tradition, see Heath, *The Mystic Way of Evangelism*. On the growing importance of the Internet as a resource for information about God, see Mike Hayes, *Googling God: The Religious Landscape of People in Their 20s and 30s* (Mahwah, N.J.: Paulist, 2007).

37 For various kinds of moral reasoning, see Robin Lovin, *Christian Ethics: An Essential Guide* (Nashville, Tenn.: Abingdon, 2000), chap. 1, which has an excellent discussion of the kind of moral reasoning that involves choosing between competing goods.

CHAPTER 3

1   Throughout this chapter, I will use the phrase "liberal Protestant" to identify a diverse group of Protestants whose theological orientation revolves around experience rather than external authority. For more on the diversity and distinguishing features of liberal Protestantism, see Evans, *Liberalism without Illusions*.

2   Bishop Will Willimon is exactly right when he insists that, far from an idea to be avoided or ridiculed, "church growth" is something to which all followers of Christ should be committed. See Willimon, *Who Will Be Saved?*, 131.

3   I am well aware that not all worship happens on Sunday morning. The image of getting out of bed on Sunday morning is simply a metaphor for the time and energy required actively to participate in the sacramental life of the church.

4   For a recent example of a Protestant theology text that treats salvation before the church, see Tyron Inbody, *The Faith of the Christian: An Introduction to Theology* (Grand Rapids: Eerdmans, 2005). For an exception to this rule, see the organization of *Essentials of Christian Theology*, edited by William C. Placher (Louisville, Ky.: Westminster John Knox, 2003). Unfortunately, while Placher manages to place ecclesiology ahead of soteriology, he also follows a tendency in many Roman Catholic systematic theologies in neglecting to include a chapter on pneumatology. For an example of this tendency in Roman Catholic systematics, see *Systematic Theology: Roman Catholic Perspectives*, 2 vols., edited by Francis Schussler Fiorenza and John P. Galvin (Minneapolis: Fortress, 1991).

5   Hans J. Hillerbrand and Helmut T. Lehmann, eds., *Luther's Works*, vol. 52 (Philadelphia: Concordia Publishing and Fortress, 1974), 39–40 (emphasis added).

6   John Calvin, *Institutes of the Christian Religion*, 2 vols., edited by John T. McNeill (Louisville, Ky.: Westminster John Knox, 1960), 4.1.4.

7   Catholic and Protestant theologians engaged in ecumenical dialogue have wrestled with these questions for many years without reaching a consensus, so we should not think we can solve all of the problems here. E.g., see the discussion in George Lindbeck's essay, "The Church," in *Keeping the Faith: Essays to Mark the Centenary of Lux Mundi*, edited by Geoffrey Wainwright (Philadelphia: Fortress, 1988), 179–208.

8   This important issue falls well outside the scope of this book. For help thinking about this matter, I recommend *Reason and Religious Belief: An Introduction to the Philosophy of Religion*, edited by Michael Peterson, William Hasker, Bruce Reichenbach, and David Basinger (New York: Oxford University Press, 2008), chap. 13. For an account that rejects the notion that all religions are ultimately the same, see Stephen R. Prothero, *God Is Not One: The Eight Rival Religions That Run the World—and Why Their Differences Matter* (New York: HarperOne, 2010).

9   This list derives from Gal 5:22-23. Other lists can be readily found throughout the New Testament, as well as in the writings of the church fathers
and subsequent theologians.

10   Boris Bobrinskoy, "Revelation of the Spirit, Language beyond Words,"
Sobornost 8 (1986): 12.

11   This notion is really just a version of the ancient Donatist heresy, which
claimed that baptisms performed by priests found to be unholy were ineffectual. In rejecting Donatism, the early church was making a profound
statement about its God.

12   Leading evangelical Protestants from outside America often stress the
instrumentality of the church in the journey of salvation. A good example of this can be seen in the life and work of John Wesley. For an account
of Wesley that lifts up his high doctrine of the church, see Vickers, *Wesley*.

13   We can see this view of salvation on display in evangelism programs that
are popular among evangelical Protestants, including the Roman Road,
Evangelism Explosion, and the like. For an approach to evangelism that
accentuates the sacramental life of the church, see Stone, *Evangelism after
Christendom*.

14   It needs to be stressed here that I am speaking only of conceptions of
and approaches to conversion that are not *intimately related to the fullness
of the church's sacramental life*. Thus the following account of theological
reductionism does not apply to all evangelical Protestant churches. On
the contrary, many evangelical Protestant traditions conceive of and
approach conversion in ways that are directly related to the sacramental
life of the church. A good example of this can be seen in the conception
of and approach to conversion in the Wesleyan tradition. See *Conversion
in the Wesleyan Tradition*, edited by Kenneth J. Collins and John H. Tyson
(Nashville, Tenn.: Abingdon, 2001).

15   Ellen T. Charry, "Augustine of Hippo: Father of Christian Psychology,"
Anglican Theological Review 88, no. 4 (2006): 577-78.

16   Charry, "Augustine of Hippo," 578.

17   What is most helpful about Charry's essay is the contrast that she draws
between Augustine's Christian psychology and modern secular psychology. The latter tells us "you can do it!" The former comes clean, admitting
that, without divine assistance, we cannot improve our situation.

18   For a more robust account of sin, see Cornelius Plantinga Jr., *Not the Way
It's Supposed to Be: A Breviary of Sin* (Grand Rapids: Eerdmans, 1995).

19   It is on this point that Sarah Coakley's work on the Holy Spirit and the
doctrine of the Trinity is especially helpful. E.g., see Coakley, "Living into
the Mystery of the Holy Trinity," 223-32. Also see the work of Martha
Nussbaum, especially *The Therapy of Desire: Theory and Practice in Hellenistic
Ethics* (Princeton: Princeton University Press, 2009).

20   On views of the atonement, see James Beilby and Paul R. Eddy, eds., *The

Nature of the Atonement (Downers Grove, Ill.: InterVarsity, 2006). Also see Paul Fiddes, *Past Event and Present Salvation* (Louisville, Ky.: Westminster John Knox, 1989).

21 For an alternative view of salvation, see Vigen Guroian, "Salvation: Divine Therapy," *Theology Today* 61, no. 3 (2004): 309–21.

22 For many people who grow up in evangelical Protestant churches, conversion and salvation turn out to be anything but easy or simple to do. E.g., see Stanley Hauerwas' refreshingly honest account of his inability as a child to "get saved" in *Hannah's Child: A Theologian's Memoir* (Grand Rapids: Eerdmans, 2010).

23 The best example here may be the work of Jim Wallis and Sojourners. While not a church, Sojourners is very influential with many evangelical Protestants.

24 A most egregious example of this can be seen in Joel Osteen and Lakewood Church, Houston, Texas. See Joel Osteen, *Your Best Life Now: 7 Steps to Living at Your Full Potential* (Nashville, Tenn.: FaithWords, 2004).

25 The doctrine of being made perfect in love for God and neighbor was one of the hallmarks of early Methodism.

26 See Kendra Creasy Dean, *Almost Christian: What the Faith of Our Teenagers Is Telling the American Church* (New York: Oxford University Press, 2010), chap. 2.

27 The overwhelming majority of United Methodist Conferences in America report statistical decline every year.

28 Letty Russell, "Why Bother with the Church?" in Placher, *Essentials of Christian Theology*, 242 (emphasis in original). For Russell's mature work in ecclesiology, see her *Church in the Round: Feminist Interpretation of the Church* (Louisville, Ky.: Westminster John Knox, 1993).

29 We will call this assumption directly into question in the conclusion to this work.

30 *NMC*'s discussion of the body of Christ, while helpful, is altogether too brief (see 7–8). A great deal more needs to be said about how we should think about the relationship between Christology and ecclesiology. Otherwise, the metaphor of the body of Christ can be very misleading.

31 The early church wrestled with this very sensibility with respect to divinity. For an excellent account of this wrestling, see Paul L. Gavrilyuk, *The Suffering of the Impassible God: The Dialectics of Patristic Thought* (New York: Oxford University Press, 2006).

32 For a helpful introduction to Christology in the early church, see Spence, *Christology*. For a more advanced account, see Oliver Crisp, *Divinity and Humanity: The Incarnation Reconsidered* (Cambridge: Cambridge University Press, 2007).

33 On brokenness and healing, see especially Andrew Sung Park, *From Hurt to Healing: A Theology of the Wounded* (Nashville, Tenn.: Abingdon, 2004).

34   In this respect, liberal Protestants are right to emphasize inclusivity, openness, and diversity.

35   The history of iconography is instructive here. Beginning in the Middle Ages, iconographers began depicting the ascended Lord of glory with wounds still bleeding. In my own Wesleyan tradition, Charles Wesley beautifully captures this in his hymn, "Arise, My Soul, Arise." After making clear that he has in mind the resurrected and ascended Lord of glory, Wesley depicts the "five bleeding wounds" of Christ as offering prayers for us today.

36   *NMC*, 10.

37   John of Damascus, *On the Divine Images*, translated by David Anderson (Crestwood: St. Vladimir's Seminary Press, 1980), p. 39 (emphasis added). John is commenting on a sermon attributed to St. Basil called "On the Martyr Gordius."

38   For more on this, see Vickers, "Medicine of the Holy Spirit."

39   This move is at the core of canonical theism, a comprehensive and international research project inspired by the work of William J. Abraham. In addition to Abraham et al., *Canonical Theism*, see Abraham, *Canon and Criterion in Christian Theology*, chaps. 1–2.

40   On any given weekend in the fall, collegiate and professional football stadiums routinely host 80,000 people.

41   In many ways, the contribution of Stanley Hauerwas has pointed out some of the concrete forms of this embodiment. E.g., see Hauerwas' *A Community of Character: Toward a Constructive Christian Social Ethic* (Notre Dame, Ind.: University of Notre Dame Press, 1981), and *The Peaceable Kingdom: A Primer in Christian Ethics* (Notre Dame, Ind.: University of Notre Dame Press, 1983). Another good example of what this embodiment looks like can be found in Paul Waddell's *Friendship and the Moral Life* (Notre Dame, Ind.: University of Notre Dame Press, 1989).

CONCLUSION

1   Deists believe that God created the universe and then stepped away, leaving it to run on its own and leaving us to rely solely on our own devices.

2   There is a great deal of debate about the very notion of the secular. Whether or not we are living in a secular or postsecular world depends largely on what one means by these terms. As I am using the term, "secular" simply denotes a widespread disposition of apathy or hostility toward religion. I take this to be the way in which the term is used most commonly among clergy and other church leaders. For a very helpful discussion of the ongoing debates about the meaning of the secular, of secularism, and of the notion of the postsecular, see Ingolf U. Dalferth, "Post-Secular Society: Christianity and the Dialectics of the Secular," *Journal of the American Academy of Religion* 78, no. 2 (2010): 317–45.

3   On the popular side, see the work of Josh McDowell.

4 The work of Bishop John Shelby Spong is a particularly well-known example of this strategy. Also, much that passes for liberation theology falls into this category. Having said this, it is worth noting that many first-generation liberation theologians did not hesitate to speak unapologetically of God, the incarnation, and the resurrection.

5 There is some evidence that scholars are beginning once again to take seriously the notion of sanctity and sainthood. E.g., see Edgardo A. Colon-Emeric, *Wesley, Aquinas & Christian Perfection: An Ecumenical Dialogue* (Waco, Tex.: Baylor University Press, 2009). In the concluding chapter of this work, Colon-Emeric makes an impassioned plea for Methodists to identify and celebrate their saints.

6 E.g., in 2006, Rutgers University (a state school!) released a report stating that its religion major and minor had tripled in size. See Rutgers University Media Relations, "Religion Studies Rise in Popularity; Rutgers Religion Majors and Minors Tripled," June 22, 2006, http://news.rutgers.edu/medrel/news-releases/2006/06/religion-studies-ris-20060622 (accessed July 19, 2010).

7 E.g., see *After Modernity: Secularity, Globalization, and the Re-Enchantment of the World*, edited by James K. A. Smith (Waco, Tex.: Baylor University Press, 2008). Also see Hunter Baker, *The End of Secularism* (New York: Crossway, 2009); and *The Desecularization of the World: Resurgent Religion and World Politics*, edited by Peter L. Berger (Grand Rapids: Eerdmans, 1999).

8 E.g., ESPN's "My Wish" segments showcase athletes who grant wishes to children with disabilities and life-threatening illnesses.

9 It is refreshing to see a leading historian of American liberalism suggest that, more than anything else, mainline liberals need to get over their obsession with taking back or saving "Christianity from the alleged sins of conservative evangelicalism." See Christopher H. Evans, *Liberalism without Illusions: Renewing an American Christian Tradition* (Waco, Tex.: Baylor University Press, 2010), 143.

Bibliography

Abraham, William J. *Canon and Criterion in Christian Theology: From the Fathers to Feminism*. Oxford: Oxford University Press, 1998.

Abraham, William J., Jason E. Vickers, and Natalie B. Van Kirk, eds. *Canonical Theism: A Proposal for Theology and the Church*. Grand Rapids: Eerdmans, 2008.

Afansiev, Nicholas. *The Church of the Holy Spirit*. Notre Dame, Ind.: University of Notre Dame Press, 2007.

Aleshire, Daniel O. *Earthen Vessels: Hopeful Reflection on the Work and Future of Theological Schools*. Grand Rapids: Eerdmans, 2008.

Ammerman, Nancy T. *Baptist Battles: Social Change and Religious Conflict in the Southern Baptist Convention*. Piscataway, N.J.: Rutgers University Press, 1990.

Anderson, Ray S. *An Emergent Theology for Emergent Churches*. Downers Grove, Ill.: InterVarsity, 2006.

Baker, Hunter. *The End of Secularism*. New York: Crossway, 2009.

Barth, Karl. *Prayer*. Translated by Sara F. Terrien. Philadelphia: Westminster, 1952.

Bauerlein, Mark. *The Dumbest Generation: How the Digital Age Stupefies Young Americans and Jeopardizes Our Future (Or, Don't Trust Anyone under 30)*. Los Angeles: Tarcher, 2009.

Beilby, James, and Paul R. Eddy, eds. *The Nature of the Atonement*. Downers Grove, Ill.: InterVarsity, 2006.

Belcher, Jim. *Deep Church: A Third Way beyond Emerging and Traditional.* Downers Grove, Ill.: InterVarsity, 2009.

Bellah, Robert N., Richard Madsen, William M. Sullivan, Ann Swidler, and Steven M. Tipton. *Habits of the Heart: Individualism and Commitment in American Life.* 3rd ed. Berkeley: University of California Press, 2007.

Berger, Peter L., ed. *The Desecularization of the World: Resurgent Religion and World Politics.* Grand Rapids: Eerdmans, 1999.

Bobrinskoy, Boris. "Revelation of the Spirit, Language beyond Words." *Sobornost* 8, no. 1 (1986): 6–14.

Borg, Marcus J., and N. T. Wright. *The Meaning of Jesus: Two Visions.* New York: HarperOne, 2000.

Bulgakov, Sergius. *The Bride of the Lamb.* Grand Rapids: Eerdmans, 2002.

Byassee, Jason. *The Gifts of the Small Church.* Nashville, Tenn.: Abingdon, 2010.

Calvin, John. *Institutes of the Christian Religion.* 2 vols. Edited by John T. McNeill. Louisville, Ky.: Westminster John Knox, 1960.

Cantalamessa, Raneiro. *The Holy Spirit in the Life of Jesus.* Collegeville, Minn.: The Liturgical Press, 1994.

Charry, Ellen T. "Augustine of Hippo: Father of Christian Psychology." *Anglican Theological Review* 88, no. 4 (2006): 577–78.

Cherry, Conrad. *Hurrying toward Zion: Universities, Divinity Schools, and American Protestantism.* Bloomington: Indiana University Press, 1995.

Claiborne, Shane. *The Irresistible Revolution: Living as an Ordinary Radical.* Grand Rapids: Zondervan, 2006.

Coakley, Sarah. "Living into the Mystery of the Holy Trinity: Trinity, Prayer, and Sexuality." *Anglican Theological Review* 80, no. 2 (1998): 223–32.

———. "The Vicar at Prayer: An English Reflection on Ministry." *Christian Century* 125, no. 13 (2008): 28–31, 33.

Coakley, Sarah, and David A. Pailin, eds. *The Making and Remaking of Christian Doctrine: Essays in Honour of Maurice Wiles.* Oxford: Oxford University Press, 1993.

Cole, Neil. *Organic Church: Growing Faith Where Life Happens.* San Francisco: Jossey-Bass, 2005.

Collins, Kenneth J., and John H. Tyson, eds. *Conversion in the Wesleyan Tradition.* Nashville, Tenn.: Abingdon, 2001.

Colón-Emeric, Edgardo A. *Wesley, Aquinas and Christian Perfection: An Ecumenical Dialogue.* Waco, Tex.: Baylor University Press, 2009.

Congar, Yves. *I Believe in the Holy Spirit.* New York: Crossroad, 1999.

Crisp, Oliver. *Divinity and Humanity: The Incarnation Reconsidered.* Cambridge: Cambridge University Press, 2007.

Dalferth, Ingolf U. "Post-Secular Society: Christianity and the Dialectics of the Secular." *Journal of the American Academy of Religion* 78, no. 2 (2010): 317–45.

Daniels, T. Scott. *Seven Deadly Spirits: The Message of Revelation's Letters for Today's Church.* Grand Rapids: Baker Academic, 2009.

Dayton, Donald W. *Discovering an Evangelical Heritage.* Peabody, Mass.: Hendrickson, 1988.

Dean, Kendra Creasy. *Almost Christian: What the Faith of Our Teenagers Is Telling the American Church.* New York: Oxford University Press, 2010.

Dodds, E. R. *Pagan and Christian in an Age of Anxiety.* Cambridge: Cambridge University Press, 1965.

Dozeman, Thomas B. *Holiness and Ministry: A Biblical Theology of Ordination.* New York: Oxford University Press, 2008.

Duin, Julia. *Quitting Church: Why the Faithful Are Fleeing and What To Do about It.* Grand Rapids: Baker Books, 2009.

Evans, Christopher H. *Liberalism without Illusions.* Waco, Tex.: Baylor University Press, 2010.

Evans, C. Stephen. *The Historical Christ and the Jesus of Faith: The Incarnational Narrative as History.* New York: Oxford University Press, 1996.

Fiddes, Paul. *Past Event and Present Salvation.* Louisville, Ky.: Westminster John Knox, 1989.

Fiorenza, Francis Schussler, and John P. Galvin, eds. *Systematic Theology: Roman Catholic Perspectives.* Minneapolis: Fortress, 1991.

Forte, Bruno. *The Church: Icon of the Trinity.* Toronto: Pauline Books, 1991.

Frejka, Thomas, and Jean-Paul Sardon. *Childbearing Trends and Prospects in Low-Fertility Countries: A Cohort Analysis.* Dordrecht: Kluwer Academic, 2004.

Gavrilyuk, Paul L. *The Suffering of the Impassible God: The Dialectics of Patristic Thought.* New York: Oxford University Press, 2006.

Gavrilyuk, Paul L., Douglas M. Koskela, and Jason E. Vickers, eds. *Immersed in the Life of God: The Healing Practices of the Christian Faith.* Grand Rapids: Eerdmans, 2008.

Groppe, Elizabeth. *Yves Congar's Theology of the Holy Spirit.* New York: Oxford University Press, 2004.

Guder, Darrell. *Missional Church: A Vision for the Sending of the Church in North America.* Grand Rapids: Eerdmans, 1998.

Gunton, Colin E., ed. *The Cambridge Companion to Christian Doctrine.* New York: Cambridge University Press, 1997.

Guroian, Vigen. "Salvation: Divine Therapy." *Theology Today* 61, no. 3 (2004): 309–21.

Hahn, Heather. "Soccer Sundays: How Do Churches Compete?" The People of the United Methodist Church website. Last modified July 2, 2010.

Accessed July 5, 2010. http://www.umc.org/site/apps/nlnet/content3. aspx?c=lwL4KnN1LtH&b=5259669&ct=8493205.

Hauerwas, Stanley. *After Christendom: How the Church Is to Behave if Freedom, Justice, and a Christian Nation Are Bad Ideas.* Nashville, Tenn.: Abingdon, 1991.

———. *A Community of Character: Toward a Constructive Christian Social Ethic.* Notre Dame, Ind.: University of Notre Dame Press, 1981.

———. *Hannah's Child: A Theologian's Memoir.* Grand Rapids: Eerdmans, 2010.

———. *The Peaceable Kingdom: A Primer in Christian Ethics.* Notre Dame, Ind.: University of Notre Dame Press, 1983.

Hauerwas, Stanley, and William H. Willimon. *Resident Aliens: Life in the Christian Colony.* Nashville, Tenn.: Abingdon, 1989.

Haught, John F. *God and the New Atheism: A Critical Response to Dawkins, Harris, and Hitchens.* Louisville, Ky.: Westminster John Knox, 2007.

Hayes, Mike. *Googling God: The Religious Landscape of People in Their 20s and 30s.* Mahwah, N.J.: Paulist, 2007.

Heath, Elaine. *The Mystic Way of Evangelism: A Contemplative Vision for Christian Outreach.* Grand Rapids: Baker Academic, 2008.

Hengel, Martin. *Between Jesus and Paul: Studies in the History of Earliest Christianity.* Eugene, Ore.: Wipf & Stock, 2003.

Hillerbrand, Hans J., and Helmut T. Lehmann, eds. *Luther's Works.* Philadelphia: Concordia Publishing and Fortress, 1974.

Hirsch, Alan. *The Forgotten Ways: Reactivating the Missional Church.* Grand Rapids: Brazos, 2007.

Holifield, E. Brooks. *God's Ambassadors: A History of the Christian Clergy in America.* Grand Rapids: Eerdmans, 2007.

Inbody, Tyron. *The Faith of the Christian: An Introduction to Theology.* Grand Rapids: Eerdmans, 2005.

———. *The Many Faces of Christology.* Nashville, Tenn.: Abingdon, 2002.

Irenaeus. "Against Heresies." Vol. 1 of *The Ante-Nicene Fathers*, edited by Rev. Alexander Roberts, Sir James Donaldson, and Arthur Cleveland Coke. New York: Cosimo Classics, 2007.

Jenkins, Philip. *Jesus Wars.* New York: HarperOne, 2010.

———. *The Next Christendom: The Coming of Global Christianity.* rev. ed. New York: Oxford University Press, 2007.

John of Damascus. *On the Divine Images.* Translated by David Anderson. Crestwood, N.Y.: St. Vladimir's Seminary Press, 1980.

John Paul II. "Post-Synodal Apostolic Exhortation of John Paul II to the Bishops, Clergy, and Faithful on Reconciliation and Penance in the Mission of the Church Today." Sec. 16. Given in Saint Peter's, Rome, December 2, 1984. www.vatican.va/holy_father/john_paul_ii/

apost_exhortations/documents/hf_jp-ii_exh_02121984_reconcilia-
tio-et-paenitentia_en.html (accessed August 12, 2010).

Jones, Tony. *The New Christians: Dispatches from the Emergent Frontier.* San
Francisco: Jossey-Bass, 2008.

Kimball, Dan. *The Emerging Church: Vintage Christianity for New Generations.*
Grand Rapids: Zondervan, 2003.

Kimbrough Jr., S. T., ed. *Orthodox and Wesleyan Ecclesiology.* Crestwood, N.Y.:
St. Vladimir's Seminary Press, 2007.

Kinnaman, David. *unChristian: What a New Generation Really Thinks about
Christianity . . . and Why It Matters.* Grand Rapids: Baker Books, 2007.

Koskela, Douglas M. *Ecclesiality and Ecumenism: Yves Congar and the Road to
Unity.* Milwaukee, Wis.: Marquette University Press, 2008.

Langford, Andy, and William H. Willimon. *A New Connection: Reforming the
United Methodist Church.* Nashville, Tenn.: Abingdon, 1996.

Lindbeck, George A. *The Nature of Doctrine: Religion and Theology in a Postliberal Age.* Philadelphia: Westminster, 1984.

Long, Thomas G. *Beyond the Worship Wars: Building Vital and Faithful Worship.*
Herndon, Va.: Alban Institute, 2001.

Lovin, Robin. *Christian Ethics: An Essential Guide.* Nashville, Tenn.: Abingdon,
2000.

MacIntyre, Alasdair. *After Virtue.* 3rd ed. Notre Dame, Ind.: University of
Notre Dame Press, 2007.

Maddox, Randy L. "Recovery of Theology as a Practical Discipline: A Contemporary Agenda." *Theological Studies* 51, no. 4 (1990): 650–72.

Maddox, Randy L., and Jason E. Vickers, eds. *The Cambridge Companion to
John Wesley.* New York: Cambridge University Press, 2010.

Martin, David. *Pentecostalism: The World Their Parish.* Boston: Blackwell, 2001.

McClaren, Brian. *Finding Our Way Again: The Return of the Ancient Practices.*
Waco, Tex.: Thomas Nelson, 2008.

McGavran, Donald A., and C. Peter Wagner. *Understanding Church Growth.*
3rd ed. Grand Rapids: Eerdmans, 1990.

McGrath, Alister E. *The Genesis of Doctrine: A Study in the Foundation of Doctrinal Criticism.* Grand Rapids: Eerdmans, 1990.

Merritt, Carol. *Tribal Church: Ministering to the Missing Generation.* Herndon,
Va.: Alban Institute, 2007.

Minear, Paul S. *Images of the Church in the New Testament.* Cambridge: Lutterworth, 2007.

Moltmann, Jürgen. *The Church in the Power of the Spirit.* Translated by Marga-
ret Kohl. Minneapolis: Fortress, 1993.

Murrow, David. *Why Men Hate Going to Church.* Waco, Tex.: Thomas Nelson,
2004.

Neuhaus, Richard John. *Death on a Friday Afternoon*. New York: Basic Books, 2000.

Newman, John Henry. *An Essay on the Development of Christian Doctrine*. Notre Dame, Ind.: University of Notre Dame Press, 1989.

Niebuhr, H. Richard. *Faith on Earth: An Inquiry into the Structure of Human Faith*. New Haven: Yale University Press, 1991.

Nussbaum, Martha. *The Therapy of Desire: Theory and Practice in Hellenistic Ethics*. Princeton, N.J.: Princeton University Press, 2009.

Oden, Thomas C. *Turning Around the Mainline: How Renewal Movements Are Changing the Church*. Grand Rapids: Baker Books, 2006.

Old, Hughes Oliphant. "Why Bother with Church?" In the *Essentials of Christian Theology*, edited by William C. Placher, 229–40. Louisville, Ky.: Westminster John Knox, 2003.

O'Malley, J. Steven, and Jason E. Vickers, eds. *Methodist and Pietist: Retrieving the EUB Heritage*. Nashville, Tenn.: Kingswood Books, 2011.

Osborne, Larry. *Sticky Church*. Grand Rapids: Zondervan, 2008.

Osteen, Joel. *Your Best Life Now: 7 Steps to Living at Your Full Potential*. Nashville, Tenn.: FaithWords, 2004.

Park, Andrew Sung. *From Hurt to Healing: A Theology of the Wounded*. Nashville, Tenn.: Abingdon, 2004.

———. *Triune Atonement: Christ's Healing for Sinners, Victims, and the Whole Creation*. Louisville, Ky.: Westminster John Knox, 2009.

Pelikan, Jaroslav. *The Illustrated Jesus through the Centuries*. New Haven, Conn.: Yale University Press, 1997.

———. *Spirit versus Structure: Luther and the Institutions of the Church*. New York: Harper & Row, 1968.

Peterson, Michael, William Hasker, Bruce Reichenbach, and David Basinger, eds. *Reason and Religious Belief: An Introduction to the Philosophy of Religion*. New York: Oxford University Press, 2008.

Placher, William C., ed. *Essentials of Christian Theology*. Louisville, Ky.: Westminster John Knox, 2003.

Plantinga Jr., Cornelius. *Not the Way It's Supposed to Be: A Breviary of Sin*. Grand Rapids: Eerdmans, 1995.

Postman, Neil. *Amusing Ourselves to Death: Public Discourse in the Age of Show Business*. 20th anniv. ed. New York: Penguin, 2005.

Prothero, Stephen R. *God Is Not One: The Eight Rival Religions That Run the World—and Why Their Differences Matter*. New York: HarperOne, 2010.

———. *Religious Literacy: What Every American Needs to Know—and Doesn't*. New York: HarperOne, 2008.

Radner, Ephraim. *The End of the Church: A Pneumatology of Christian Division in the West*. Grand Rapids: Eerdmans, 1998.

Regele, Mike. *The Death of the Church.* Grand Rapids: Zondervan, 1996.

Reno, R. R. *In the Ruins of the Church: Sustaining Faith in an Age of Diminished Christianity.* Grand Rapids: Brazos, 2002.

———. "Out of the Ruins." *First Things* 150 (2005): 11–16.

Russell, Letty. *Church in the Round: Feminist Interpretation of the Church.* Louisville, Ky.: Westminster John Knox, 1993.

———. "Why Bother with the Church?" In *Essentials of Christian Theology,* edited by William C. Placher. Louisville, Ky.: Westminster John Knox, 2003.

Russell, Robin. "Claremont's Religious Diversity: Church Affirms Multi-Faith Project." *United Methodist Reporter,* July 2, 2010. http://www.umportal.org/article.asp?id=6914 (accessed August 18, 2010).

Schmemann, Alexander. *For the Life of the World.* Crestwood, N.Y.: St. Vladimir's Seminary Press, 1995.

Shorto, Russell. "No Babies?" *The New York Times.* Last modified June 29, 2008. Accessed July 7, 2010. http://www.nytimes.com/2008/06/29/magazine/29Birth-t.html.

Slaughter, Michael. *Change the World: Recovering the Message and Mission of Jesus.* Nashville, Tenn.: Abingdon, 2010.

———. *Unlearning Church.* Nashville, Tenn.: Abingdon, 2008.

Smith, James K. A., ed. *After Modernity: Secularity, Globalization, and the Re-Enchantment of the World.* Waco, Tex.: Baylor University Press, 2008.

———. *Thinking in Tongues: Pentecostal Contributions to Christian Philosophy.* Grand Rapids: Eerdmans, 2010.

Soskice, Janet Martin. *Metaphor and Religious Language.* Oxford: Oxford University Press, 1987.

Spence, Alan. *Christology: A Guide for the Perplexed.* London: T&T Clark, 2008.

Stark, Rodney. *What Americans Really Believe.* Waco, Tex.: Baylor University Press, 2008.

Stone, Bryan. *Evangelism after Christendom: The Theology and Practice of Christian Witness.* Grand Rapids: Brazos, 2007.

Sullivan, Francis. *From Apostles to Bishops: The Development of the Episcopacy in the Early Church.* Mahwah, N.J.: Paulist, 2001.

Van Dyk, Leanne, ed. *A More Profound Alleluia: Theology and Worship in Harmony.* Grand Rapids: Eerdmans, 2004.

Vergara, Camilo. *How the Other Half Worships.* New Brunswick, N.J.: Rutgers University Press, 2005.

Vickers, Jason. "Albert Outler and the Future of Wesleyan Theology: Retrospect and Prospect." *Wesleyan Theological Journal* 42, no. 2 (2008): 56–67.

———. "Charles Wesley's Doctrine of the Holy Spirit: A Vital Resource for the Renewal of Methodism." *Asbury Theological Journal* 61, no. 1 (2006): 47–60.

———. *Wesley: A Guide for the Perplexed*. London: T&T Clark, 2009.

Viola, Frank. *Finding Organic Church: A Comprehensive Guide to Starting and Sustaining Authentic Christian Communities*. Colorado Springs: David C. Cook, 2009.

Volf, Miroslav. *After Our Likeness: The Church as the Image of the Trinity*. Grand Rapids: Eerdmans, 1998.

Waddell, Paul. *Friendship and the Moral Life*. Notre Dame, Ind.: University of Notre Dame Press, 1989.

Wainwright, Geoffrey, ed. *Keeping the Faith: Essays to Mark the Centenary of Lux Mundi*. Philadelphia: Fortress, 1988.

Wainwright, Geoffrey, and Karen B. Westerfield Tucker, eds. *The Oxford History of Christian Worship*. New York: Oxford University Press, 2005.

Ward, Pete. *Liquid Church*. Peabody, Mass.: Hendrickson, 2002.

Warren, Rick. *The Purpose Driven Church*. Grand Rapids: Zondervan, 1995.

Weaver, J. Denny. *The Non-Violent Atonement*. Grand Rapids: Eerdmans, 2001.

Webber, Robert. *Ancient-Future Faith: Rethinking Evangelicalism for a Postmodern World*. Grand Rapids: Baker Books, 1999.

Webster, John. *Holiness*. Grand Rapids: Eerdmans, 2003.

Willimon, William H. *Who Will Be Saved?* Nashville, Tenn.: Abingdon, 2009.

Wilson-Hartgrove, Jonathan. *New Monasticism: What It Has to Say to Today's Church*. Grand Rapids: Brazos, 2008.

Wittgenstein, Ludwig. *Philosophical Investigations*. 3rd ed. Translated by G. E. M Anscombe. New York: Macmillan, 1953.

Wolterstorff, Nicholas. *Justice: Rights and Wrongs*. Princeton: Princeton University Press, 2010.

World Council of Churches. *Confessing the One Faith: An Ecumenical Explication of the Apostolic Faith as It Is Confessed in the Nicene-Constantinopolitan Creed*. Rev. ed. Eugene, Ore.: Wipf & Stock, 2010.

———. *The Nature and Mission of the Church: A Stage on the Way to a Common Statement*. Geneva: World Council of Churches, 2005.

Yeago, David. "The New Testament and the Nicene Dogma: A Contribution to the Recovery of Theological Exegesis." *Sewanee Theological Review* 45, no. 4 (2002): 371–84.

Index